Before the War &
After the Union
by Sam Aleckson

AFRICAN AMERICAN

LITERATURE SERIES

The earliest African American writings frequently bore witness to the trauma of the slave trade, resistance to bondage, and fight against oppression, but these literary expressions also reflected cultural traditions created by fusing African, European, and American artistic practices. As the tradition developed, writers embraced multiple genres, including songs, poetry, sermons, speeches, narratives, antislavery tracts, letters, and petitions. This series, the first university press series devoted to the African American literary tradition, invites proposals for monographs, edited collections, and annotated editions that feature innovative new research from a variety of historical, theoretical, and critical perspectives.

Series editors

Valerie Babb, Emory University
Rhondda Robinson Thomas, Clemson University

Before the War &
After the Union
by Sam Aleckson

Written by
SAMUEL WILLIAMS
with an Introduction
and Annotations by
SUSANNA ASHTON

CLEMSON
UNIVERSITY
PRESS

First Edition, 2021

ISBN: 978-1-949979-83-1 (print)
eISBN: 978-1-949979-84-8 (e-book)

Published by Clemson University Press
in association with Liverpool University Press

Clemson University Press is located in Clemson, SC.
For more information, please visit our website at www.clemson.edu/press.

Library of Congress Cataloging-in-Publication Data

Names: Aleckson, Sam, 1852-1946? author. | Ashton, Susanna, 1967- editor,
writer of introduction.
Title: Before the war & after the union / by Sam Aleckson ; written by
Samuel Williams ; with an introduction and annotations by Susanna
Ashton.
Other titles: Before the war and after the union
Description: [Clemson, South Carolina] : Clemson University Press, [2021] |
Includes bibliographical references and index. | Summary: "Sam Aleckson
was the pen name for Samuel Williams, a man born into slavery in
Charleston, South Carolina, who wrote a memoir about his life and the
world around him during and after his bondage. Published privately by
his family, Before the War and After the Union traces Williams's life
from his earliest memories of being enslaved and forced to serve
Confederate soldiers in army camps, through the post-Civil War years as
his family struggled to re-connect and build a new life during
Reconstruction. It the ends with tales about his life as the head of a
southern Black family newly relocated to Vermont at the
turn-of-the-century"-- Provided by publisher.
Identifiers: LCCN 2021011773 (print) | LCCN 2021011774 (ebook) | ISBN
9781949979831 (paperback) | ISBN 9781949979848 (ebook)
Subjects: LCSH: Aleckson, Sam, 1852-1946? | Slaves--South
Carolina--Charleston--Biography. | Freedmen--South
Carolina--Charleston--Biography. | African Americans--South
Carolina--Charleston--Biography. | LCGFT: Slave narratives.
Classification: LCC E185.97 .A34 2021 (print) | LCC E185.97 (ebook) | DDC
306.3/62092 [B]--dc23
LC record available at https://lccn.loc.gov/2021011773
LC ebook record available at https://lccn.loc.gov/2021011774

Typeset in Minion Pro by Carnegie Book Production.
Printed and bound in Poland by BooksFactory.co.uk.

Contents

Figures

Acknowledgments

It was an initial team of lively and inquisitive students in my Clemson University Creative Inquiry course on South Carolina slave narratives from 2008 to 2009 who assisted me with the conception of *"I Belong to South Carolina"* as a collection of South Carolina narratives featuring an author we then only knew as Sam Aleckson. I thank them for the labor and their love. That initial team of industrious students was made up of Robyn E. Adams, Maximilien Blanton, Laura V. Bridges, E. Langston Culler, Cooper Leigh Hill, Deanna L. Panetta, and Kelly E. Riddle, and I am grateful for all their hard work.

My next acknowledgment must go to the descendant of Samuel Williams who went to the trouble of writing me a letter in 2010 after reading about my collection. I am deeply ashamed that I misplaced that letter and have no record of your name. In your letter you revealed to me that the author's name truly was Samuel Williams. That revelation was enormous. It took a few years to play out, but this book project was instigated by your kindly engagement with me back then. I hope someday we manage to connect and I hope that your South Carolina branch of the family can see in this project the honor and respect I have for the way in which your witty, wry, and hard-working ancestor lived his life and shared his truly American story.

Williams's descendants through his daughter Susan are aware of this project and through Erika McClain as their emissary have shared details about his life and the wonderful photograph of him and his grandson

(Fig. 1). Their pride in their family history and their willingness to share what they knew about his life has been invaluable and this work is dedicated to their family. If there are any royalties from this project, I shall direct them entirely to the International African American Museum in Charleston in the name of Samuel Williams and his descendants.

A second group of students in the spring of 2016 helped me unpack a new version of Williams's life, once I actually knew his true name. Thank you for all the help from Glenn Bertram, Kristen Doe, Vanessa Eggenschwiler, Clare Kelly, Melissa Knapp, Kirsten Alexandra Nelson, Hannah Thompson, Mary-Kate Tilley, Lydia Wardlaw. Special gratitude is due to Hannah Meller and Benjamin Barkley who stuck with the project as research assistants long after the semester ended. They braved freezing cold explorations in Charleston, painful adventures with InDesign and Wikipedia, and then finally helped out with the broader plan for what evolved into the exhibit for the Lowcountry Digital History Initiative for the Lowcountry Digital Library at the College of Charleston. Benjamin Barkley even took time out from a vacation in Vermont to visit where Williams lived in Windsor (Fig. 2).

The Charleston team with the Lowcountry Digital History Initiative helped me imagine this project from early on. It started with encouragement and lively conversations with Mary Battle. And when she left to discover other opportunities, the project was next taken over by Leah Worthington, who provided me with cheerful guidance though many months of my confusion over the tasks at hand. I'd never before conceived of a life story played out as a text-heavy digital exhibit. It was educational and humbling to learn what a specialized medium this mode of public history is.

Librarians and curators at the Vermont History Society helped me fact check and understand much of Williams's life in New Hampshire and Vermont. I still have many speculations about his life that riff off inadequate although promising evidence but any errors in that vein are entirely mine. Especial thanks to Marjorie Strong, who went beyond any reasonable expectations in the digging she did for me.

My interest in the dressing table owned by the Waring family was a bit inchoate but the very patient Daniel K. Ackermann, Interim Chief Curator at the Old Salem Museums & Gardens took time to answer many of my questions about its provenance and significance.

1 Samuel Williams and his grandson

Elizabeth Adams and Andrew Hnatow worked on the footnotes and indexed with creative and scholarly brio and Alison Mero patiently guided this project along through all of its stages. I especially appreciate her patience in listening to me talk thought the extraordinary and confounding nature of this coded work.

I also thank my many good friends and colleagues in Charleston who often met me for an encouraging lunch or coffee when I'd visit the city for research. Simon Lewis and Scott Peeples advised me about Charleston opportunities, and their friendship has been enriching and sustaining

2 Photograph of Thomas family house on Main Street, Windsor, Vermont, where Williams lived and worked

both to my scholarly life but also to my personal sense of what long-term friendships can reap.

Clemson University has assisted me with this project in a number of ways. Thanks to the Clemson University's Creative Inquiry program I have been able to build this project over a decade. You really don't know much about something until you teach your way through it and the opportunity to involve students in these mysteries of Williams's life has brought us all a long way. Support came from the Clemson University Digital History foundation led by Vernon Burton, which recognized the value of my work and ended up helping fund the work for the Lowcountry Digital History exhibit. It bears mentioning, too, that the library and staff at the Clemson Universities Libraries, especially Camille Cooper, have been unrelentingly generous and patient with their time and assistance.

Finally, I thank my family for their good cheer and kind support.

Editor's Notes

Racial Terminology

When editing and framing historical materials for contemporary readers, particularly when those materials confront head-on the racial attitudes and mores of a broken world, we must ask questions about audience and effect as well as exploring issues of intentionality and the nuances of what kinds of critical analysis are deployed within the work itself. In the case of *Before the War and After the Union*, Samuel Williams does himself not just invoke but directly addresses the use of what I shall refer to here as the "n— word." I thus have chosen to leave his language as presented, in part because his analysis is precisely about the word itself and how it resonates for a Black man when coming from the mouth of a white man in turn-of-the-twentieth-century New England. Other racialized terms such as "buckra" are glossed in the footnotes and, significantly, are used by Williams differently for white and Black people in different contexts and so merit close readerly attention.

Dialect

The presentation of dialect in this narrative can offer challenges and opportunities for readers, just as any other form might, but the dialect here is pretty consistently done, and once you work your way through a phrase or two you should be able to notice those common phrases repeated. For example:

"gwine" = going
"bime by" = by and by.

The rule of thumb when reading dialect is usually to try to figure words out from context and, when possible, to simply try saying those sentences aloud. One passage in Chapter VI discussing Union Major Robert Anderson's surrender of Fort Sumter reads: "Genlemen, if I had food fer my men, an ambunachun I be dam if I wud le yo cum en dose gates!" which might look a bit disconcerting to the inexperienced reader but when read aloud can be understood as "Gentlemen, if I had food for my men, and ammunition, I would be dammed if I would let you come in those gates"

As Editor, I have resisted "translating" any of his dialect passages because they are true to his memory and any such translation would belie the point he is trying to make about the humanity of his community that exists, even when the expression of that humanity is alien or alienated from the culture of oppressors. The dialect might initially obscure a bit of meaning for the contemporary reader (although traditions of dialect fiction were so well established in the late nineteenth and early twentieth centuries that Williams's imagined audience of the 1920s would certainly have been somewhat accustomed to the language). But, in the same way his use of coded names and misdirected locales positions white readers just a bit outside of their comfort zone when reading a memoir of Black lives, and conveys to the white reader that they shouldn't be overly confident in their mastery of the tale or in their interpretative control of the narrative, Williams's use of dialect simultaneously and cleverly matches up with expectations for genres of regional fiction of the time. It also pushes readers permanently outside of the walled courtyards or plantation labor camp boundaries. One of the effects of Williams's dialect passages is to slyly question the confidence readers, whether historical or contemporary, and whether white or Black, might have in their own interpretations. By discomfiting any confident translations, he allows his enslaved speakers to have, at least in his memory, a bit of their cultural privacy assured.

Literary Invocations and Epigraphs

Williams's interest in literacy and education is a recurring theme, which also provides us with a context for understanding his use of dialect. His own prose is conversational and smooth with only occasional disjointed segues or misordered plot points, a fact that should not be surprising for a partly blind author in his sixties drafting informal sketches for what was to become a family published book. With a few exceptions, he generally assigns white individuals standard speech forms that align with how he, as a Black narrator, speaks.

Williams's own education was a bit uneven, as he explains in his narrative—he was tutored by the Jones sisters when he was young and by 1870 the Federal census identifies him as fourteen years old and as a student "at school." Williams doesn't mention any other formal education but his appreciation for the early learning he received is demonstrated by a letter he wrote in 1915 that was reprinted across various Black newspapers. In this letter he shared his memories of the Jones sisters, lauding them for how they might serve as models for the quality of instruction and love that white teachers could provide for Black children, despite the push at that time to segregate educators teaching students of different races.

The tutoring from the Jones sisters, and a few years of possible education in Charleston after the war aside, the bulk of his education was likely self-driven after his teens, and while he was undoubtedly working tremendously hard to support his family throughout his life, it is tempting to speculate that during those long, dark Vermont nights he and his family read aloud together. I share this speculation because it would help explain the enormous number of literary references he speckles throughout his text. From children's nursey rhymes to hymns, he recreates for readers what might have been a soundscape as much as an imaginative space for his life. His references to Shakespeare and many poems that seem to have been regular items in recitation and schoolbooks also hint at the fact that his children may have brought home and shared books from the wonderful Springfield, Vermont school system he so praised.

Later, when Williams was employed by and living with the affluent Carter family of New Hampshire, and even more so when he was caretaking for the Thomas family of Vermont (headed by Thomas H. Thomas, a man who reported himself to the 1920 census as an "Author" whose industry was "Books"), it is plausible to imagine Williams and his daughter Susan enjoyed access to books and periodicals made available to them in such surroundings. I have sought to source as many of Williams's quotations, epigraphs, and literary references as possible in order to build out a frame for us to better understand the contexts of his composition and the breadth of his cultural imagination.

Williams's book was self-published by his grandson's press that appears to have been established for legal documents and not book publication. Indeed, by 1930, Williams's grandson's profession was listed as a "typesetter" in the Federal census, so it seems likely he had typeset the manuscript for his grandfather. The physical book itself was small, poorly bound, and laid out in a rather idiosyncratic manner, perhaps an illustration of its homespun origins.

In only three or four places in this entire manuscript have I silently corrected obvious typographical errors or otherwise emended the text to facilitate presentation. Many other textual errors or exceedingly minor accidentals remain, and sometimes in the dialect passages it can be hard to discern what is intentional and creative shaping of words versus what might be typesetting mistakes. And yet, since they are part of the flavor and perhaps the intent of the author, I let them stand so long as they didn't impede on the readability of the text.

The People

While many names are referenced in this memoir with varying levels of detail, the particular nature of the identities that were coded and disguised in Williams's extraordinary memoir demands a bit more interrogation and presentation than the footnotes alone can show. The list of names, below, imperfect though it may be, describes individuals in the order that they are first mentioned in the text and includes analysis and speculation about what their actual names and identities might have been. Since some of the historical figures, such as General William Tecumseh Sherman, are references made broadly by Williams that don't reflect his inner circle, I have kept these as contextual footnotes for the master narrative but have not listed them here in "The People," which is designed more as a directory of Williams's own world.

Name	Notes on identities and speculations
The author: Sam Aleckson	"Sam Aleckson" is a pseudonym for Samuel Williams, who asserted his copyright on the first edition of this volume in 1929. His father's name was Alexander Williams.
Great grandfather, Clement	Clement Williams would have been Williams's great-grandfather's name and, as noted by Williams, Clement was presumably or possibly enslaved by a white family named Williams at some point in time.
Father	Alexander Williams (?1823–99)
Mother	Susan Williams (?1825–95). Williams names one of his daughters Susan, after his mother.
Brother	Samuel Williams's older brother died as a child during the Civil War while laboring under a Confederate officer.
Grandmother	It is presumably Samuel Williams's father's mother that is referenced in his memoir here, since, at other points, Williams explains that he was largely in the care of family members from his father's side. This would have been quite unusual because the ownership of enslaved children would usually be with the owner of the enslaved mother.
The three ladies	These three sisters he refers to as the "Jaynes" were undoubt-edly the three Jones sisters of Guignard Street: Elizabeth, Sarah, and Susan. Elizabeth died in 1857 but the other two ladies continued living in Guignard Street during the period Williams depicts. Sarah and Elizabeth Jones are both buried in the cemetery ground of the Circular Church of Charleston. One of them may have owned and enslaved Alexander Williams or had some other intricate family connection with the enslavers of Susan or Alexander Williams that evidently allowed for young Samuel Williams to be under their care.
Jennie	An enslaved childhood friend.
Miss S	Either Sarah or Susan Jones, referenced in the first chapter of the memoir.

Name	Notes on identities and speculations
Mrs. Dane	Possibly Anna Deas Samuel's mother's enslaver. Anna Deas may have been originally married to a member of the Waring or "Ward" family but remarried into the Deas or "Dane" family. These relationships are a bit speculative, but they seem to fit the contours of Williams's narrative and the historical record. If she is the daughter of "Mrs. Dane," as Williams says, that means she was probably Anna Waring Turner, a daughter of Mrs. Dane's (Anna Deas's) first marriage.
Mr. Thomas Dane	Thomas was possibly also Edward Waring (not Dane), the son from a first marriage of Anna Deas. This was possibly a stepson of Anna Deas or "Mrs. Dane."
Mr. Edward Dane	Thomas might also have been a name for Edward Waring (not Dane), the son from a first marriage of Anna Deas.
Mrs. Turner	If she is the daughter of "Mrs Dane," as Williams says, that means she was probably Anna Waring Turner, a daughter of Mrs. Dane's (Anna Deas's) first marriage.
Aunt Beck	A woman enslaved by "Thomas Dane."
George	The son of Aunt Beck. He was sold by "Thomas Dane," who was probably a member of the Deas family.
Uncle Renty	A man enslaved by the "Dane" or Deas family.
Mrs. Bale	Probably a member of the Boyle family or possibly the Ball family, both prominent clans in Charleston, with many properties in and around the Lowcountry of South Carolina.
Mrs. Ward	Most likely Mrs. Waring, who would have been "Mrs. Bale's" daughter (or a Mrs. Ball or Boyle's daughter). She and her husband now and then lived with "Mrs. Bale." Since Joseph Hall Waring II, the most likely identity of "Mr. Ward," married a Rosa Wilson Schultz in 1858, and since she was part of a Boyle family and they married at a cousin, Mary Boyle's house, we can see that the Waring/Boyle or "Ward"/"Bale" connections are confusing but quite credible.

Name	Notes on identities and speculations
Tom Bale	"Mrs. Bale's" son and thus possibly named Tom Boyle.
Cora	Cora appears to have been the daughter of one of the enslaved laborers held by the "Bale" or Boyle family.
Uncle Ben	An enslaved man who worked as a coachman for the "Wards" (likely the Waring family).
Joe and Hector	Older boys also enslaved by the "Ward" or likely the Waring family.
Sandy	Another enslaved boy or man on the "Ward" plantation labor camp.
Mr. Ward	Probably Joseph Hall Waring II (1823–76), a large slaveholder with extensive family connections throughout South Carolina. He served in Company K, 4th South Carolina Cavalry, which was sent to Virginia during the Civil War. He was a State Senator in 1865. He owned Pine Hill and Clayfield Plantation labor camps in Dorchester County, South Carolina. Pine Hill was likely what Williams refers to as "Pine Top."
Jake	Another young, enslaved person at the "Pine Top" labor camp.
Uncle Sempie	An older enslaved man who served as a butler to the "Ward" family.
Mingo	A man enslaved at another local plantation labor camp within walking distance of "Pine Top." He visits to spend time with Dolly, the woman he later marries. The fact that he is not owned by "Mr. Ward" and yet at a later point in this narrative "Mr. Ward" directs him to be whipped goes unremarked in this memoir but is a notable demonstration of the absolute power white enslavers had over Black people regardless of the chain of ownership.
	A Black man named "Moses Hudson" appears in the 1880 Federal census as living in Kershaw, South Carolina (not far from the area where the "Pine Top" property would have been) with a wife Millie and a young boy named Mingo Hudson. It seems possible that Millie might be "Dolly" and Moses could have been "Mingo" in the narrative.

Name	Notes on identities and speculations
Mr. Hudson	Mingo's enslaver.
Dolly	The daughter of Josh and Peggy and later became a wife of Mingo.
Uncle Josh	The father of Dolly.
Aunt Peggy	The mother of Dolly. She continued to serve "Mrs. Ward" after the war.
Uncle Joe	"Mr. Ward's" driver or overseer.
Aunt Binah	Uncle Joe's wife.
Uncle August	An enslaved man who worked closely with "Mrs. Ward."
Mr. Brabham	A carpenter and friend of the "Ward" family who was included in their hunting party event.
Mr. Benton	A neighbor of "Mr. Ward."
Aunt Lucy	An enslaved woman who worked as a nurse.
Manda	An enslaved housemaid.
Mr. Boyleston	Many people named "Boyleston" lived in the Lowcountry region of South Carolina, but it is possible this was Henry Boyleston, an enslaver based in Charleston, who, according to the 1860 Federal slave schedule, held nineteen slaves.
York	Enslaved coachman to "Mr. Boyleston."
Titus and Pompey	"Mr. Ward" uses these enslaved men to protect his property.
Dick Brown	A knowledgeable fisherman skilled in the Lowcountry waterways.
London	An enslaved coachman working for Mr. "Bale" (or Mr. Boyle).
Ceasar	An enslaved man
Silla	A woman enslaved by "Mrs. Tom Bale."
Brother Jim	Silla's brother perhaps, or perhaps a free Black laborer in Charleston who had money to give her gifts.
Aunt Cinda	An elderly enslaved woman.
Miss Octavia	Octavia appears to have been the first name of "Mrs. Tom Bale." She was a tormenter of Silla.

Name	Notes on identities and speculations
Mrs. Bate	Perhaps proprietress of a boarding house. This might have been a Mrs. Bates.
Mr. William	A brother of "Mr. Ward." Possibly Mr. Waring.
Mr. Bennett	"Mr. Ward's" or possibly Mr. Waring's brother.
His wife	H. Williams was Samuel Williams's second wife. Since his first wife Mary Artsen Williams died in the mid-1880s, he likely married shortly thereafter. She may have had children from an earlier marriage.
Children: Tom, Dick, Harry, Betsey Ann, Matilda Jane	These are not the real names of his children. Some of the children he is referring to may be children from his previous marriage, children with his second wife, or perhaps stepchildren. His first child with Mary Artsen Williams died as a baby in 1880. According to this letter, he evidently had several other children, including Susan, with whom he seems to have lived the last forty years of his life. He also had a son Samuel B. Williams Jr. and a daughter Carrie E. Williams, who all are listed with their older sister Susan as living with him (and without their mother or stepmother) in the Windsor City Directory of 1905.
G	It is hard to speculate here but "G" was possibly a relative of Williams who had suggested he come to Vermont, or perhaps G was a relative of Williams's second wife.
Miss M	A welcoming Vermont resident.
Mrs. B	A Vermont neighbor.
Old man who lived nearby	This elderly neighbor told Williams about the local church.

Introduction

In 2010, a few weeks after my third child had been born, I received a handwritten letter. I am ashamed to admit that in some sort of post-partum haze I misplaced it almost immediately after reading it and lost the details about the sender, but I remember the gist of it well.

It was a fan letter of sorts! This correspondent had tracked down my address to say that they had seen the media coverage concerning my recently published collection of South Carolina slave narratives (*"I Belong to South Carolina": South Carolina Slave Narratives*, 2010).

"I was so happy to see that your book was featuring the memoir of Sam Aleckson," I recall the letter saying. It continued by revealing (and I very roughly paraphrase from memory): "He was my Great, Great Uncle. My family knows about his book, but we never knew anyone else knew about it as well. Of course, his real name was Samuel Williams, as you probably know." Um, no. I had not been aware that his real name was Samuel Williams, and even though the copyright of the book was clearly assigned to Samuel Williams, I had carelessly and vaguely attributed that to being the name of some sort of possible patron or amanuensis and had allowed myself to set aside that vital clue without much consideration!

I share this story of scholarly process in all of its humiliating truth because I think there are lessons to be learned here about community, about humility, and about how to ask questions in new ways. And, even more importantly, this revelation opened up what is perhaps one of the most curious artifacts of life writing about the practice of slavery and its aftermath.

I had edited a somewhat shortened version of what I then thought of as the "Aleckson" memoir in my *"I Belong to South Carolina"* collection and while I had attempted with my team of student researchers to gather a bit of background information and context analysis on "Aleckson," we had turned up very little about the author of this compelling but unmoored memoir that alternated between charmed nostalgia and harrowed memories. But now, knowing the author's real name, thanks to the descendant I still have not been able to trace and properly thank, I had a vital tool to unpack a richer and deeper story than I ever could have anticipated.

And, with his true name, Samuel Williams, some harder and utterly unanticipated truths could finally be untwined. With a new group of students, I launched investigations into his life and work and eventually drew upon that collaborative to create a digital exhibit hosted by the Lowcountry Digital Library at the College of Charleston. The digital exhibit showcased many of the archival treasures that illuminated Williams's life and featured many pictures and text and even an interactive timeline to walk folks through his long and complicated life. Nonetheless, the nature of the exhibit still could not provide the intense and intimate textual experience of actually reading his memoir and understanding its particular challenges and insights.

Thus, in this volume I build on the work undergirding the exhibit to present a version of *Before the War and After the Union* with copious annotations, not merely to fill out truths and identities previous scholars (including myself) had not uncovered. The motivation behind this new edition is to do more than naming names and identifying persons long dead. The reason to reshape this narrative for modern readers is to understand the reverberations and stakes of naming names. For with this astonishing memoir Samuel Williams inverts the fraught history of the Black archive.

As most scholars of African American history can attest, traditional approaches or strategies for archival research often require reading into the margins. Scholars seeking to trace the lives of people of color, particularly before the first Federal census to list the names of African Americans in 1870, have long had to seek out missing pages, parse real estate inventories, unpack land transactions, or examine plantation labor camp receipts in order to imaginatively extract the individual stories obscured by the inhumanity of archival annihilation. Any scholar who has worked with tax inventories from Southern states in the antebellum era, for example, is familiar with the Federal slave schedules which meticulously record the human property of every enslaver by age and sex but do not deign to reference names or family units.

And so, when working with life writing of former slaves, or looking into the diverse history of our nation's Black history, scholars have had to reconstruct a history that is often coded and obscured. What is astounding about Samuel Williams's memoir, therefore, is that, for the most part, he works to obscure the white history of the enslavers. He himself uses a fake name as the author (although not on the copyright page, which clearly asserts "Samuel Williams" as the copyright holder). And yet, the names of most of the Black people he was enslaved with, the community members who sustained, mentored, tormented, shaped, and survived alongside him … for the most part Williams constructed his story to let them shine, to allow their names to come forth.

In this way, as contemporary readers, we may not be certain who, say, "Mrs. Boyle" was (although I provide careful and historically informed speculations about such matters in my notes and directory of The People), but we can be confident that the stories of Mingo, Dolly, or Silla are told in a way that is designed to highlight their truths.

In this light, we can see that even Williams's own code name of "Aleckson," which so confounded me early on, is ridiculously simple to decode once you understand who Williams was and what his values were: he was the son of Alexander Williams, the family patriarch who managed, after the Civil War, to bring a scattered family back together. Even while using a false name, Williams calls out to his father.

With these trickster-style reversals, Williams, via his twentieth-century memoir, turns upside down the scholarly histories of the slave narrative genre. We can think of his work in a slyly modernist context that is worth unpacking in a discussion of where and how he wrote his book in the editorial center of the modernist publishing world. But, more powerfully, we can think too of this memoir as reframing the early twentieth-century nostalgia for halcyon plantation tales. His warm anecdotes may evoke loving memory at times, but they are always framed in fear and displacement. Whether it was fears of retaliation towards his relatives still in Charleston or whether it was a general apprehensiveness about riling up difficult memories in an era when lynchings and violence were a constant, Samuel Williams could not, even in 1918 or so when he drafted his narrative, risk a full reckoning.

There are many possible reasons Williams may have altered and disguised the names of so many white families that were powerful players in his life story, even though he was writing some fifty years after emancipation. He may not have wished to offend them or reveal intimate details the current descendants might not have appreciated; he may have wished to protect his own family members still living in Charleston from retribution; he might have wanted to embroider stories with impunity; he might have simply forgotten or misspelled some of the names; and, most of all, whether consciously or unconsciously, he might have wished to effectively recenter the story upon his own experiences and the experiences of his family members.

To be clear, Williams does not present his work as fiction. Nonetheless, the careful practice of allowing one's memoir to be both detailed enough to be plausible and yet vague or obscurantist enough to mask its precise truth is not unknown among memoirs written during the era of slavery (Harriet Jacobs's *Incidents in the Life of a Slave Girl*, published in 1861, is perhaps the most famous example of this). The obscurity he particularly deploys when referencing white individuals in his narrative, whether he feared them or admired, thus allows for focus—his memoir thereby centers around his own story and the insights he provides about his own vision of the complex world around him during and after slavery.

In my introduction here, I draw upon my work designing the digital exhibit for the Lowcountry Digital History Initiative for the Lowcountry Digital Library at the College of Charleston, *Samuel Williams and his World*, to illustrate and frame out for readers some of the most telling structures and incidents of his life, some of which were described in his memoir and some of which rely upon external research I have pursued to understand the parts of his life he left out from his story.

Despite the fact that he wrote his memoir as an elderly man in Vermont, far from his birthplace in South Carolina, Samuel Williams's memoir, spanning from the 1850s to 1914, provides rich insights into his early life in Charleston, the complex world of urban slavery, and the struggles and achievements of Williams and his family following emancipation. His memoir includes glimpses into the labor of enslaved children in Charleston in the mid-nineteenth century, from working as jockeys in horse races for the entertainment of white gamblers to forced service for the Confederacy. After the Civil War, a teenage Williams stayed in Charleston and attended school. It might have been the Avery Normal Institute, a well-known private school for Black students in Charleston at the time, but there are no extant records to confirm his enrollment there. It might also have been at the Morris/Simonton School, also in Charleston, a public institution for African American children that also required fees but was less elite than the Avery Normal Institute.

Either way, however, his family must have worked hard to ensure that their smart and ambitious teenager had opportunities to advance. Over time, young Williams found work with local businesses, including work as a porter, and soon achieved enough financial stability to marry and start a family. The 1880 census indicates that Williams married a local seamstress in Charleston, Mary Artson. They had a baby son who died shortly after birth. To compound his sufferings, Williams then became a widower when Mary died in the early 1880s. Despite the sorrow of these years, by 1888, Williams had remarried. Though his memoir provides few details about his marriages or his children, this second wife may have had children by an earlier marriage, and the couple also went on to raise children of their own.

With a growing family to support, Williams moved north for better opportunities. Unlike many African Americans of this era who moved to urban industrial centers such as New York or Detroit, somehow Williams found an attractive position in Vermont. He doesn't chronicle how this happened—was it a newspaper advertisement, word of mouth from a white patron? A tip from a Black laborer? It is difficult to speculate too much on this matter. But we do know that it was a life-changing decision. Shortly after he arrived and settled himself, he sent for what appears to be his second wife, possibly named Henrietta,[1] to join him with their

---

1   See *Before the War and After the Union*, Chapter III n. 13.

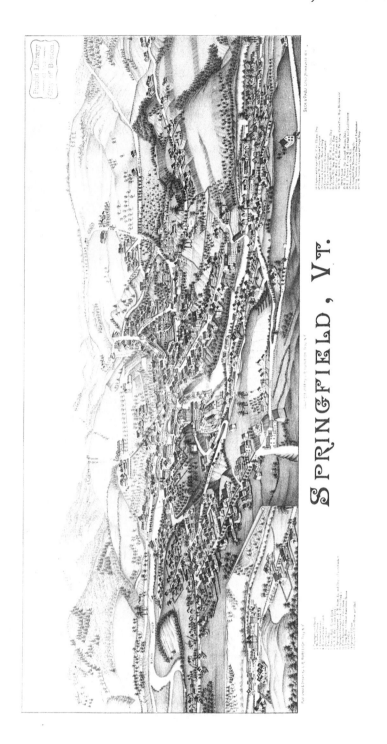

3 Map of Springfield, Vermont, c.1886

4 Campbell Carter house, Lebanon, New Hampshire, *c*.1910

children, and they settled into their new lives, first in Springfield, Vermont, and then in various other locations throughout Vermont, New Hampshire, and Massachusetts (Figs. 3 and 4). By the early twentieth century, it appears that his second wife died or left, and Williams apparently spent the rest of his long life living with his eldest daughter Susan. Concerned about his life, legacy, and failing eyesight, he decided to write down his memories. While working as a live-in house servant, Williams found time to sketch out the story of his life from 1852 up through 1914.

Throughout his memoir, Williams bears witness to major historical events, such as the Great Charleston Fire of 1861 and the hotly contested South Carolina gubernatorial election of General Wade Hampton in 1876. He also lingers on more personal memories, such as his early education with a group of white women on Charleston's Guignard Street who taught him to read. In New England, he recalls his astonishment at encountering the abundance of pie in the region. Ultimately, his narrative weaves together a moving story of survival, community, and courageous perseverance. As Williams's title reveals, while slavery was "Before the War," but carving out a life "After the Union" also demands recognition. His memoir is a remarkable and rare account of the Civil War and its Reconstruction aftermath from the perspective of a man who was raised as property but survived to proclaim his own life story as testament to his humanity. Williams lived for several decades after he penned his 1914 narrative, and he most likely passed away in Massachusetts in the mid-1940s. Archival evidence suggests that he continued to have a rich life beyond the years documented in his memoir and maintained a strong relationship with extended family members who cared for him as he aged.

The Narrative

The long tradition of African American writing includes many genres, but it is perhaps the nineteenth-century autobiographical tradition that most influenced the course of contemporary African American literature. Within this autobiographical tradition, the writing of what have been traditionally termed as "slave narratives" by survivors of enslavement but now are referred to with more nuance as "freedom narratives" dominates the popular imagination and cultural understanding of the Black experience in the United States from the mid-seventeenth to the mid-twentieth centuries.

Today, the term "slave narrative" in North America can broadly refer to twentieth-century interviews with survivors, eighteenth-century confessions by enslaved people who had been jailed for rebellion or arrested for one reason or another, and seventeenth-century captivity or religious-conversion narratives.

For most scholars, however, the term is usually limited to first-person accounts, either composed or dictated by individuals who directly endured legal bondage and who told of the experience of enslavement as a defining part of their life experience. While there is no hard and fast rule, the most important criterion is whether an account is by someone who has survived being enslaved. While the term is applied to narratives written as far back as the eighteenth century, North American slave narratives most commonly refer to narratives written during the era of abolition (roughly 1830 to 1860) or composed in the four decades following the Civil War.

Many twentieth-century narratives are better understood as "interview narratives" that were assembled and transcribed over the years. The most significant interview collection is that of the Federal Writers' Project of the Works Progress Administration (WPA), which includes some 2,300 interviews with African American survivors conducted between 1936 and 1938. This collection provides invaluable first-hand accounts of enslaved life, but these accounts were often not constructed by the interviewees on their own terms, and therefore suffer from limitations as historical texts. As verbal interviews, government workers often erratically transcribed these accounts, and many of them were simply brief answers to structured questions. Due to the timeframe of the interviews (conducted during the 1930s), the interviewees were people who had experienced slavery as children, with few direct memories and impressions of the institution as an adult. That, coupled with the power imbalance between predominantly white interviewers hired by the Federal Writers' Project and their elderly Black interviewees—who were often impoverished in the context of the Great Depression and in need of government assistance—meant that WPA narratives can appear skewed. Many accounts include nostalgic or relatively benign memories of slavery, in stark contrast to far more brutal and horrifying accounts of slave life given by those who experienced the institution as adults, and who were able to tell their story without mediation from white government actors. While the experiences of slavery were ultimately diverse and individual, the historical contexts of how and when "interview narratives" took place are critical for understanding what shapes different accounts.

Samuel Williams wrote his memoir well after the era of antebellum abolitionist narratives, but also a full generation before the Federal Writers' Project's interview narratives. His work, however, shares qualities from both traditions. In addition, his work is a literary text arising from the written tradition rather than from a recorded interview. He does recount anecdotes of his youth with some warmth and seems to consciously play down many of slavery's horrors, much like many interviewees for the Federal Writers' Project. Significantly, though, his story also seeks powerfully to connect enslaved life to an experience of struggle and survival, through Reconstruction and into the early twentieth century.

As a first-hand account of his life shaped by the system of slavery, Williams's memoir can certainly fall into a traditional definition of the slave narrative or freedom narrative—particularly that of the postbellum era. It is particularly intriguing to speculate whether he was familiar with Booker T. Washington's enormously successful memoir, *Up From Slavery* (1901), which chronicled a similarly ascendant life arc, framed by optimism and confidence in the rightness of the American people and the promise of a new century. In later years, when Williams moved in with his daughter Susan, who had successfully married into the professional class (she married a man who worked as both a dentist and as a lawyer and who lived in a townhouse in Cambridge), we can see the astonishing way in which Williams's hard work and sacrifices could be framed into a story akin to the well-known saga of Booker T. Washington's ascendancy.

Whether wholly original or somewhat stock, Williams's life story was told with a relentless emphasis upon community and how an individual's story could only be understood as part of a whole.

With the exhibition that inspired this project, and now with the rich annotations provided here, we can begin to contextualize and build out his life story and that of his family. But what is also key is that by understanding the breadth of his life a bit more than his standing among other memoirs, we can better see what life was like for enslaved and formerly enslaved people during his lifetime, and we can also better understand how individuals who had to depend upon one another to survive interlocked their stories with one another.

Though he was emancipated as a young teenager, Williams demonstrates that his life story could never be separated from his own bondage, nor separated from the impact that slavery had on the people around him. Williams tells his own story, but he dedicates even more space to telling the stories of the people who did not have the opportunities that he had. He bears witness for those who died in slavery or soon afterwards, shares stories of people who were illiterate and destitute, and recounts a story of slavery that decentralizes himself in favor of a broader community that he identified with.

Writing and Publishing the Memoir

Williams's memoir has a unique publication history. Written later than most nineteenth-century abolitionist-era slave narratives and later even than the next generation of post-bellum narratives of the second half of the nineteenth century, he did not complete the manuscript draft until after 1914, by which time he was approximately sixty-two years old. It was not published until 1929. It is hard to know why he and his family were uninterested in securing or unable to secure a publisher for so many years, but we can speculate that he might have approached some people with literary connections and found both inspiration and discouragement.

His own account of the memoir's composition is a bit vague. As he recounts it, he was advancing in years and feared that he was going blind (this was likely between 1914 and 1920, or so). Hence, he wanted to write his life story down while he still could:

> When I began this unpretentious narrative, I was almost sight-less. I had just recovered from a severe attack of illness, during which for a time I became totally blind, and after I was better my eyes seemed hopelessly affected…. . My life had not been wholly uneventful; I had been of an observant turn of mind from my youth. What if I could set down the events that had come under my observation in some connected form? Might I not thereby be able to earn something to ward [sic] my support when I could no longer see!

Sometime after 1914, Williams finished his manuscript for *Before the War and After the Union*, chronicling his life up until 1914, during which time he closed out his story living with his daughter as an in-home servant for a prosperous family in Windsor, Vermont. It wasn't until 1924, or so, though, that Williams revisited his manuscript, and it was published in 1929 with Gold Mind Press, a business created by his son-in-law and grandson. This private press appears to have existed primarily for printing legal documents and only ever appears to have produced this one book.

While the story of Williams's illness provides some insight into the emotional urgency of the project and might also explain why, upon his recovery, he was less concerned with doing anything with the text, there are still many questions about what might have happened during those years. For Williams had some surprising and fortunate connections with the literary world which might well have influenced both its construction and its failure to find a publisher.

The situation is this: During the years between 1914 and at least 1920, or so, Williams worked for families along the New Hampshire and Vermont border, and as Federal Census data indicates, he was certainly employed by the Thomas family of Windsor, Vermont, as a live-in servant by 1920, if not before. Since his memoir lists the location of its composition as Windsor on its title page, it seems probable that he wrote his book while living with the Thomas family.

This job may have proved serendipitous, for, by chance, Williams had ensconced himself into the house of a man with tremendous literary connections. Thomas Head Thomas was a Harvard-trained art historian and author and the brother-in-law of Maxwell Perkins, the most famous editor of literary America in the early twentieth century (editing works by Ernest Hemingway, Thomas Wolfe, and F. Scott Fitzgerald). Since Perkins also maintained a summer house in the small town of Windsor during these years, we can reasonably imagine that the two closely related families interacted with one another a great deal; interactions of which Williams would have certainly been aware. To be sure, Williams never mentions Thomas, much less Perkins. And there is no evidence that either Thomas or Perkins knew of, much less encouraged or advised, Williams in any way on his personal manuscript. Nonetheless, that Williams and his grown daughter Susan were living in a house run by an author with myriad prominent publishing and literary connections does raise some tempting conjectures.

Williams was almost certainly not living with the Thomas family when he started his memoir since it seems that family was abroad during much of World War I and Williams isn't listed as living with them until the census of 1920. And his own account suggests he at least began his narrative sometime in or shortly after 1914. Nonetheless, if he held onto his notes or his drafts through the period in which he began living with the Thomas household, it does raise some speculative questions. Did he ever mention to his employer that he had an unpublished manuscript of his life? Did he receive discouraging responses from his employer and his influential publishing circle? Did he receive encouragement, only to be still unable to place his memoir with an editor? It is hard to imagine that Thomas and his brother-in-law Perkins would not have been able to offer useful advice if they were aware of and wished to encourage Williams's writing. We may never know. But the fact that this modestly educated yet sharply inquisitive and reflective man took it upon himself to pen the story of his life in order to bear witness to his experiences before his eyes might fail him surely reflects upon the fact that he was living in a house where words mattered, and books were currency.

Whatever the reason, Williams's unpublished manuscript remained within his own family and did not appear in print until 1929, long after his Windsor sojourn had ended and he was living in Cambridge, Massachusetts. It took his own Black family to bring his story out to the world. It appears that it took Susan's husband and her stepson to finance and arrange for its publication under an imprint of their own creation, Gold Mind Publishers of Boston. This means that Williams's book was not published with the help of a white-owned gatekeeper or publishing house, or even with the introduction or endorsement of an influential white guarantor. Rather, the 1929 publication illustrates the family's determination and faith in the importance of Williams's testimony.

The memoir's appearance through an independent publisher may also help explain why it is such a distinctive manuscript. As a privately produced work, brought into the world by a family of Black professionals, the memoir did not have to adhere to any vetted agenda for white publishers, such as comforting white audiences with purely nostalgic memories of plantation life. Instead, the work reflects Williams's own complex experiences, needs, and perspectives. Even when his reflections seem nostalgic, he also hedges. For example, his description of "Mr. Ward at Pine Top" is revealing. While Williams notes that "Mr. Ward" was "what was called a 'good master,'" and that "His people were well-fed, well-housed and not over-worked," he also carefully adds that, for this enslaver,

> There were certain inflexible rules however, governing his plantation of which he allowed not the slightest infraction, for he had his place for the Negro. Of course the Negro could not stand erect

in it, but the Negro had no right to stand erect. His place for the Negro was in subjugation and servitude to the white man.

Ultimately, Williams makes his views on slavery clear in his memoir:

> There is nothing good to be said of American slavery. I know it is sometimes customary to speak of its bright and its dark sides. I am not prepared to admit that it had any bright sides, unless it was the Emancipation Proclamation issued by President Abraham Lincoln.

Before the War and After the Union bears witness to many experiences and lives discarded, passed over, ignored, destroyed, and repurposed. In its modest way, Williams's tale is an effort to reinsert a voice of power over a dark past.

Enslaved Childhood in Charleston

Walking through an interpretative introductory reading of his entire narrative is an enormous task but in the sections that follows I have attempted to gloss at least some of the notable events and incidents in his life that are referenced in detail or in passing in his life story in order to highlight some of the most surprising, atypical, or telling ways in which his story stands out from many other survivors' autobiographies. And one of the standout aspects of his story is the lengthy emphasis he puts upon his urban childhood and his experiences before the war, which occupy the bulk of his memoir.

In 1852, Samuel Williams was born in Charleston, South Carolina. According to his account, his grandfather was Clement Williams, a man whose name was created for him upon his arrival from Africa sometime in the late eighteenth century. Clement Williams's descendants, including his son Alexander and grandson Samuel, proudly retained this last name. Samuel was one of at least five children born to an enslaved couple, Susan and Alexander Williams, and today the descendants of the Williams family live across the United States in California, New York, Massachusetts, and South Carolina.

With Samuel Williams's parents enslaved by different households in Charleston, his family did not consistently live together until after the Civil War. And, as with many families of enslaved persons, it is a bit difficult to clearly track the legal ownership of various people throughout their lives. During his early years, young Samuel Williams lived with his parents, grandmother, and four siblings—Alexander (Jr), Louisa, Alice, and Robert—most regularly with the owners of his father, a family he calls "The Danes." At various points in his young life, though, Williams's family was forced to shuffle between different households to benefit the finances or simply the convenience of their enslavers. Williams recollects for some years only being able to see his mother on Sundays because she was hired out to a white family who allowed her to see her children only once a week. Around the age of nine or ten, Williams's mother was sold away from Charleston; he did not see his mother again until after the war.

While there are, so far, no extant or known images of his parents, a photograph of Williams from the 1940s (see p. xi) suggests he was relatively fair skinned in complexion. In addition, according to the 1870 census, by 1870, in the post-war era, Alexander Williams held a position as "Keeper of Tidal Drains," which was a city-sponsored position that required filing reports and hence suggests he was literate. Moreover, the apartment the family occupied by 1870 on Princess Street was in a neighborhood largely occupied by the Black artisan class. These various factors hint that the Williams family may have experienced easier access to socioeconomic opportunities during slavery and after emancipation. In the racial hierarchies of Charleston, lighter skin could translate to higher-class standing within Black communities, allowing greater potential access to education and employment after slavery, particularly in Charleston's urban context. But, of course, the Williamses were still vulnerable to the abuses of the slave economy and racial prejudice following emancipation. Whatever security they constructed could always be undermined by their white enslavers and later white employers and cultural or legal restrictions.

Williams's life in bondage as a child in Charleston differed in various ways from the experiences of enslaved children in more rural areas, though they shared the unjust terms of forced labor. Slavery on rural plantation labor camps in the surrounding Lowcountry region usually demanded arduous agricultural work; slavery in urban contexts also required forced labor, as well as uncomfortably close contact with white slaveholders. This regular proximity with whites had violent physical and psychological consequences for enslaved people. At the same time, in cities like Charleston, enslaved people had some access to greater mobility and independent trade markets and networks within Black urban communities. As Williams's life illustrates, however, such advantages often came at a price.

In both urban and rural contexts, enslaved men, women, and children were vulnerable to the perpetual insecurity of being treated as chattel property by their owners. And, while Williams has many warm recollections of his childhood in Charleston in the 1850s, the horror of his separation from his mother and his accounts of the cruelties he witnessed remain etched in his mind. These vignettes of trauma are often scattered throughout otherwise cheerful anecdotes in his memoir, but they indicate dark scars of suffering lasting throughout his life story.

Literacy

It should not be surprising that most narratives written during or after the war included some discussion of how the author had learned to read or at least how the author had been forbidden to learn. This served the purpose of helping authenticate for a white audience, who were evidently the gatekeeping powers of racist skepticism, that the narrative was genuine. Even more so, though, it was usually included to demonstrate the singular importance of education in helping the enslaved individual embrace themselves as mentally and intellectually free, even when their bodies were not under their own control.

In the opening of his memoir, Williams explains, "I began to write at night often under poor light, being scarcely able to see the words as I traced them. Thus my MS. [manuscript] was finished." But how and when did Williams learn to read and write? The answer to that question is one of the most remarkable revelations of his story.

Many such narratives chronicle a harrowing struggle to gain access to literacy with secreted books or illegal lessons shared by the firelight, but—incredibly—Williams was taught to read and write by a group of white women who either owned his father or were part of a household the Williams family was affiliated with. While South Carolina laws during the time of Williams's youth forbade teaching enslaved or free people of color to read, even more important than the technical law itself was that the dominant cultural mores of the period were emphatically opposed to anyone of color being educated. As Williams noted in his memoir, an enslaved person caught with a textbook could be "severely punished."

Williams refers to the sisters who taught him to read as the "Misses Jaynes." Williams also notes the women attended the Circular Church in Charleston. Research pulled from city directories, census data, and church membership of the 1850s and 1860s produces a trio (and after the death of one, a pair) of unmarried white women—Sarah, Susan, and Elizabeth Jones—living together in a house on Guignard Street. The Jones sisters also attended, and two of them were later buried at, the Circular Congregational Church, and they were almost certainly Williams's teachers. It is difficult to know precisely the motivations behind his early classes with the sisters, but according to Williams's narrative the "Misses Jaynes" evidently taught young Williams alongside Jennie, another enslaved child, using a textbook he identifies as the Reverend Mr. Thomas Dilworth's *A New Guide to the English Tongue*. As Williams writes:

> We had only one book each, but it was a great book…. From it, like all great men, we first learned our A B C's, then came A-b-âb, B-ā, ba and so on to such hard words as ac-com-mo-da-tion, com-pen-sa-tion and the like…. and many a slave was severely punished for being found with a copy of it in his hands.

Dilworth's book was often used for instruction in the United States from the eighteenth century onwards, but by the time Williams encountered it in the late 1850s, it would have been outdated—the final edition was published in 1827. With that significant time lapse in mind, it seems likely he was taught by the "Jayne" sisters from one of their own childhood schoolbooks.

Even if his beloved Dilworth was outdated, the rudimentary education he received enabled Williams to go on to more structured schooling after the Civil War. We do know that he was listed as "at school" in the 1870 census, so he did receive some formal education beyond those early experiences.

In later years, Williams held up his early educational experiences with the Misses Jaynes as an argument about the efficacy of cross-racial education. In 1915, in defending the right of white teachers to teach Black children (a contested question at the time), he wrote to a newspaper that "it was my good fortune to have as teachers three ladies ... and when I was about to leave school it was one of these who grasped my hand and bade me godspeed."[2]

Williams's love and praise for these three sisters notwithstanding, his observation about the harsh punishments enslaved people could receive if discovered with a book makes clear that he found these remarkable opportunities to learn amidst a culture of surveillance and oppression. In this article, as in much of his memoir, he carefully balances genuinely warm memories with strategic depictions of tremendous injustice and suffering.

His Experiences as an Aspiring Child Jockey

In memories of his youth, Williams cheerfully recalls frolicking with white "playmates," running with family dogs, and climbing fig trees. While Williams's own memories with his young friends are positive, it was not uncommon for enslaved children to be used as playmates or entertainment for white children until their enslavers determined their utility shift directly to labor. Moreover, even his most positive memories are troubling in their implications. For example, Williams remembers the excitement of riding horses as a child jockey, while entertaining white audiences at great risk:

> My mother and her children fell to the lot of Edward Dane, brother of Thomas. This young gentleman was of a gay disposition; fond of horses and the sports of the day.... . He taught me to ride, and when I could sit my horse well "bare-back" he had

2   While he probably initially wrote to a Black newspaper in New England with his thoughts, it isn't clear which one it would have been. His letter was republished, though, and appeared in several other venues, including the version I quote here. See Samuel Williams, Oakland, California, "Samuel Williams' Views," *Oakland Sunshine*, September 14, 1915 (accessed through Readex).

5 Photograph of Charleston Racecourse clubhouse, *c*.1865

a saddle made for me at the then famous "McKinzie's" saddlery, sign of the "White Horse at the corner of Church and Chalmers Street. (Gentlemen had their saddles made to order in those days). I would often accompany him "up the road" on horseback to the Clubhouse, there to exhibit my youthful feats of horseman-ship, for the divertissement of Mr. Dane and his friends.

Horse racing was a central part of American sporting culture in the nineteenth century. Charleston, in particular, served as a hub in the ante-bellum period, and the city's annual Race Week attracted citizens from all over the country (Fig. 5). Williams would have been familiar with the festivities, and he was convinced that Edward Dane, his enslaver, was training him to ride with the hopes of using young Williams as a jockey, only to have the plans dashed by the onset of the Civil War and a cessation to such entertainments.

Being an athlete, even one still held in bondage, might have seemed an exciting opportunity for a young boy, as opposed to many other fates that

RUINS OF THE CIRCULAR CHURCH, ON MEETING STREET, CHARLESTON, S. C.—SEE PAGE 312.

6 Ruins of the Circular Church on Meeting Street, Charleston, South Carolina

could have awaited him, but all enslaved people, from those who labored in the fields to those trained as jockeys, were still subject to brutal treatment and physical risk. In his memoir, though, Williams recounts feeling a sense of satisfaction with his childish athleticism, and he takes pride in his exploits as a horseman, proclaiming that he and his horse Agile "never had a mishap."

The Great Fire of Charleston and the Breakup of His Family

On December 11, 1861, a massive fire devastated Charleston. Effectively destroying over 500 homes and the livelihoods of many of the city's inhabitants, this fire burned prominent local institutions such as the Circular Church (Fig. 6) and Institution Hall. In Williams's memoir, he describes the destruction of Charleston, including his former home on Guignard Street, as "the greatest conflagration that has happened in Charleston during my lifetime." Memories of the fire were still fresh decades later. Williams recalls, "The sparks seemed to rain down from the heavens as we ran." He further details how firefighters tried to douse the flames, but largely failed, leaving behind a "mass of ruin." Williams goes on to relate the destruction of the Roman Catholic Cathedral, whose "costly and magnificent edifice melted away" under the flames of the fire.

Perhaps due to the devastating fire coupled with the deprivations of the Civil War, or perhaps due to other issues, the family that owned Williams, his mother, and his siblings were in difficult financial straits. As a result, they made a calculating and cruel decision to separate the Williams family. In an understated manner typical of Williams, he explains that when the "Dane's" bankrupt estate was preparing for sale, the enslaved people they owned were summoned for "appraisement," young Williams included. He recalls being confused by how sad all of the enslaved people looked even though they were dressed in the finest clothes.

> Several gentlemen came out into the yard. The people stood up, and the gentlemen went among them asking questions. One of them placed his hand on my head... . "Well, my boy," said he, "What can you do?"
>
> "I can ride, Sir," I answered, whereupon my mother gave me a gentle nudge which meant, "Hush." She then explained to him that my brother and I were not to be sold for she had earnestly requested Mr. Dane not to "sell" us. She knew that we should receive good treatment as long as we were in his hands, and that if we went with her, the Negro Traders would soon separate us. With many protestations Mr. Dane had promised her that he would not sell us even if he had to go barefoot. He kept his word, but my mother and two little sisters went and for four years, we neither saw nor heard of each other.

Although his mother and sisters may have remained in South Carolina, the cruelty of forced separation from his family appears to have shaped how he treated and constructed his own family years later—we know he sought to bring all his children to Maine, and, as an adult, Williams prioritized family above all and labored throughout his life to keep his own children cared for and his family intact.

Life on "Pine Top"

As described by Williams, the onset of the Civil War brought financial upheaval to the "Dane" family. Whether it was because of general financial panic, the great Charleston Fire of 1861, the loss of northern investments, or perhaps failing banks, the "Dane" family fell upon hard times. To generate funds, in the time before they actually started selling off people under their power, the "Danes" hired out Williams's mother Susan to work as a cook in the home of a widowed woman in Charleston whom Williams calls "Mrs. Bale." According to Williams, the widow's daughter was married to a man with the surname "Ward." The "Ward" family owned what Williams refers to as "Pine Top Plantation" (Fig. 7). Williams's recollections of life at this site make it evident that the "Dane," "Bale," and "Ward" families were incredibly entwined in sharing, selling, and hiring one another's human property over the next few years. While young Williams does not seem to have, technically, actually been owned or enslaved by the "Ward" family, he was absolutely under their control for long stretches, and he spent several months at the Ward family "Pine Top" plantation labor camp on and off during the Civil War. While it isn't entirely clear in his narrative how these chains of bondage were variably attached to the different white families in his life, the fact that he was always under the control of the whims and nego-tiations of white families was not atypical of the lives of enslaved people, who were frequently mortgaged, lent, leased, rented, or borrowed as the interests of their enslavers dictated.

Williams's written memories of "Pine Top" feature a mixture of beau-tiful and violent scenes, but his initial introduction opens with a rich description of the plantation's landscape. The combination of his youth and his outsider status on the "Pine Top" plantation labor camp might have been contributing factors to his initial romantic recollections of its environs:

PINE TOP, Mr. Ward's country seat, was a beautiful plantation about eighteen or twenty miles from Charleston. The house, an

7 Blue cabin on the Waring family's "Pine Top" (or Pine Hill) Plantation labor camp in Dorchester County, South Carolina

old colonial mansion, stood on elevated ground, well back from the main road, and commanded a fine view of the surrounding country. From the main road the house was reached through a wide avenue, lined on either side by giant live oaks, while immediately in front of the house was a large lawn circled by a wide driveway.

From the front door of the house the barns, stables, gin-house, corn mill and Negro quarters, presented the appearance of a thriving little village. The quarters were regularly laid out in streets, and the cabins were all whitewashed.

As with many references in his narrative, Williams appears to have obscured the identity of the site by creating a false name. Quite likely, however, he was referring to Pine Hill plantation labor camp near the Ashley River, which was owned by a branch of the prominent Waring family. Records suggest that "Mr. Ward" was actually Joseph Hall Waring II (1823–76), owner of Pine Hill plantation labor camp in Dorchester County, who served as a

State Senator in 1865, fought with the 4th Regiment South Carolina Cavalry (known as "Butler's Brigade"), and was a prominent citizen of Summerville, South Carolina. Like many of the white people mentioned in Williams's carefully crafted memoir, altered names and coded references do not allow us to identify "Mr. Ward" with perfect confidence and thus Williams's strategic narrative obscurantism is quite effective in placing the emphasis upon his own beloved family and his own experiences, and displacing the prominent white people from the center of the memoir.

Williams's stories of "Pine Top" primarily describe the exchanges between enslaved adults and "Mr. Ward." He chronicles how such interactions could begin genially but end with violence and cruelty. Williams depicts the paternalistic and oppressive regime "Mr. Ward" imposed upon enslaved people under his control. For example, Williams writes of a chilling incident involving Mingo, an enslaved man from another property. Mingo had to ask "Mr. Ward" for permission to visit a "Pine Top" woman, Dolly, after first getting specific permission from his own master. Slave passes were provided by white people to validate the movement or presence of enslaved people when off their enslavers' land or away from direct supervision. These notes were a precarious form of protection, since they could be lost or destroyed, and their language was often left up to the interpretative interests of the reader. This could prove dangerous to the pass recipient, as Mingo was to discover.

When "Mr. Ward" found Mingo visiting Dolly with a pass bearing no specific destination, "Mr. Ward" instructed his slave driver: "Mingo has forgotten my orders. Take him over to the barn and give him twenty lashes." It appears this violence was unleashed upon Mingo because "Mr. Ward" assumed Mingo was not only visiting Dolly but unfaithfully visiting women at other plantations as well. Whether the permission letter was not worded in a manner Mr. Ward found specific enough or for another reason young Williams did not catch, the enslavers' violent actions against enslaved people was their prerogative. Thus, to uphold "Mr. Ward's" own sense of propriety and paternalistic power, Mingo, not legally under "Mr. Ward's" control, was tortured.

As Williams tells it, Mingo defied "Mr. Ward's" offensive presumption by persisting in his courtship, eventually marrying Dolly, and living with her long after the Civil War brought them freedom. Nonetheless, the story illustrates the careful way Williams weaves together nostalgia and witness testimony. He praised "Pine Top's" comparatively generous food and provisions ("Mr. Ward was what was called a 'good master.' His people were well-fed, well-housed and not over-worked") but still calls attention to the intrusive and violent presence of "Mr. Ward" in the personal lives of people in his bondage. As a young boy, Williams did not have to receive the twenty lashings to understand that his life was controlled by the same violence that controlled Mingo. Williams's bearing witness to Mingo's and Dolly's experiences speaks to the variety of ways in which enslavement impacted the human experience. Everyone on "Pine Top" would have known that "Mr. Ward's" violence towards Mingo was invoked to control and terrorize them all.

Secessionville

One of the most extraordinary parts of this memoir, and one which truly sets it apart as a rare historical resource, is Williams's recollections of his experiences as a child laborer, forced to serve the Confederacy.

Williams's older brother (a child of thirteen, perhaps) was sent along as a private slave to serve "Edward Dane." This officer took the young boy to Secessionville, an army encampment on James Island outside of Charleston, and the boy evidently contracted some sort of camp fever and died. Young Samuel, who was probably only ten or eleven years old at the time, was then sent in his place:

> I took my brother's place as officer's boy! And here I must admit I wore the "gray." I have never attended any of the Confederate reunions. I suppose they overlooked my name on the army roll!

Williams's bitterly ironic tone in this excerpt indicates that his service should be understood in its correct context: that of the forced slave labor of a child. As with all tasks that Williams's enslavers forced him to comply with, his Confederate service speaks to his lack of freedom and choice. The time he spent laboring for a Confederate officer is not an indication of his loyalty to the Confederacy but rather an indication that the Confederacy utilized enslaved people, even young children, to carry out their war.

With wry understatement, Williams places his own tragic family history counter to the false nostalgia people still express about loyal slaves willingly serving the Confederacy. In his case, it was the death of his older brother Alexander that directly led to his service under Confederate officer "Edward Dane." These assignments exposed his brother and later Williams to the illness and pestilence of military camp life. As Williams sadly remembered of his brother, "the dear boy contracted fever and soon died."

Williams was thus forced to travel to the James Island encampment of Secessionville, outside of Charleston. He ran errands, waited upon "Mr. Dane," and occasionally made trips from the island to the city to fetch and deliver clean laundry. Williams never experienced any battles directly, although he did witness Union bombardment, death, and the brutal treatment of enslaved workers.

Enslaved men were forced into serving the Confederate forces throughout the South. Between 1862 and 1864 alone, over 4,000 enslaved men were forced to labor around the Charleston area sites where they were compelled to defend and rebuild fortifications and defenses on Sullivan's Island, James Island, and Fort Sumter, among other places. Some of these men were worked to death or died of disease in these abysmal working conditions. While Williams and his brother were likely sent as private slaves and not part of any formal war tribute to the Confederate government, the effect was the same: they were coerced under threats of violence to support the goals of their oppressors.

Williams's account reminds us not only how horrifying the encampments and battles must have been for a child, but, conversely, how his child's perspective also colored his insights at that time. "My duties were light," he tells his readers, and, as an old man recollecting events, he seems to be unsure himself how to reconcile his joy at adventure with the desperate horror he saw. To owners of human property in the South, the enslaved men and children who died while under Confederate control were primarily seen as financial losses. Some of the planters, members of the Confederacy themselves, sent letters to the Confederacy requesting reimbursement for their "property" losses. However, to the families of enslaved men and children, these deaths were personal and tragic. Williams's own mother and father, of course, lost their son, Alexander. And Williams lost his older brother.

Freedom and Reconstruction

The Union Army marched into Charleston on February 18, 1865, and many who marched were members of the 21st Regiment Infantry of United States Colored Troops. They enforced the Emancipation Proclamation and only with this Federal presence, when Charleston was taken from Confederate control, could Williams finally obtain his freedom. In his memoir, Williams embraces a then-derisive term, "Sherman Cutloose," with pride to honor the Union general who helped bring about his emancipation.

> I shall have to admit that I was a "Sherman Cutloose" (this was a term applied in derision by Some of the Negroes who were free before the war,—To those who were freed by the war). I am Persuaded however that all the Negroes in the slave belt, And some of the white men too, were "Cutloose" by General Sherman.

After the war ended, Williams joined a crowd of freed people to greet Union Major General Anderson when he returned to Charleston to raise the Unites States flag over Fort Sumter. The significance of this event made an impression upon him inasmuch as we can tell from his discussions about Anderson's significance in his storytelling about the import of Fort Sumter during the war years.

Still, building a new life was an uncertain venture for freed people after the war. The first thing Williams did, like so many newly freed people, was seek out his family members from whom his enslavers had separated him. In 1861 or 1862, Williams's mother Susan and his younger sisters Louisa and Alice had been sold away from their original enslavers—and therefore away from the rest of their own family—to an unnamed location. Williams wrote that while he and his brother stayed on through the war years with "Mr. Dane," he was not able to see his mother and sisters again until the end of the Civil War. It is unclear in the memoir where Williams's father, Alexander Williams, was during the war years; but one way or another, and likely through great difficulty (although Williams doesn't discuss it), shortly after the end of the Civil War, the Williams family was finally reunited and living together in one household.

8 Page from the 1880 Federal census showing the Williams family together at 5 Princess Street, Charleston, South Carolina

No. *1 . 2 0* RECORD for *Samuel Williams* .

Date, *May 2. 1871 e*
Where born, *Charleston S e*
Where brought up, *do*
Residence, *5 Princess St*
Age, *18 y* Complexion, *Brown*
Occupation, *Porter*
Works for *Office on Broad St*
Wife or Husband,
Children,

Father, *Alexander Williams a*
Mother, *Susan Williams*
Brothers and Sisters, *Robert C, Alice, Louisa*

REMARKS:

Signature,. *S. Williams*

9 Freedman's Bank account record for Samuel Williams, 1871

And thus a new era began for the family. From 1868 to 1884, the complete Williams family (mother, father, younger sisters, Samuel, and his brother) appears in the city directories and census records as part of a single household on 5 Princess Street in Charleston (Fig. 8). And now that they were together, for the next decade or so, life seems to have improved for the family. As they were no longer considered chattel property, the family members could be recognized with the dignity of a documented civic presence. Both Alexander Williams and Samuel Williams opened bank accounts with the Freedman's Bank (Fig. 9).

10 Pages from the 1877 Charleston voter registration book

Williams and all other newly freed people quickly found that freedom was not given over easily by the white power brokers of the era. He spends time in his narrative to reflect on the racial inequality codified through the oppressive Black codes which were passed immediately after the war by white Southerners, which affected the lives of all Black South Carolinians. Though slavery was legally abolished with the Thirteenth Amendment to the United States Constitution, white Southerners utilized these new sets of laws to restrict the social and legal rights of African Americans. Black codes included statements, for example, restricting freedom of movement for Black laborers without permission of their employers. And while newly freed people like Mingo and Dolly no longer needed a slave pass to see each other and were finally allowed legally to marry after the Civil War, Black codes in South Carolina still restricted their movement by requiring "the master" (landowner) to give them permission to leave the property. Though they were legally free, white control over Black bodies remained part not only of South Carolina law but of state laws across the United States.

As Williams was surely acutely aware, the era of Reconstruction presented tenuous citizenship to newly freed Black Americans. The Thirteenth Amendment did indeed end legal slavery in 1865 and, in 1870, the Fifteenth Amendment did secure Black Americans the right to vote. However, neither amendment halted white people's attempts to continue to assert power over newly freed people. Nor did Black people stop resisting this control. While many Black codes were specifically designed to circumvent the Fifteenth Amendment and stop Black people from registering to vote, in 1877, Alexander and his son Samuel Williams nonetheless took the bold move doing just that. Their names and addresses were written down by the precinct officer, which was then copied into a Charleston election ledger. And while we do not have a record of Williams or his father actually voting, both of their names appear in the 1877 Charleston election precinct ledger as citizens and eligible voters (Fig. 10). It would take many other newly freed people decades or longer to feel safe taking the same step.

Life in Vermont and New Hampshire

The Great Migration of African Americans from the South to the North, Midwest, and West from the late nineteenth to the late twentieth centuries typically involved movement to cities for jobs and a desire to escape the constraints and violence of Jim Crow segregation. While Williams's account of moving North is peaceful, white racism and acts of violence increased as American cities saw an influx of Black people. Over this time period, the nation saw a shift from having 90 percent of Black Americans living in the South to having almost half of Black Americans living outside of that region. Samuel Williams left South Carolina in the late 1880s, placing him at the vanguard of this great population shift. It must have been an uncertain venture during an uncertain time.

In his memoir, Williams does not reveal exactly what drew him to Springfield, Vermont (which he refers to in his narrative as "Spring Lake, Connecticut). It was certainly a state with a long history of abolitionist support and was the first state in the nation to ban slavery with their 1777 prohibition against human bondage. There is no mention of this fact in his memoirs, though, so perhaps it was just a fortuitous opportunity of some sort that came his way. He does describe a "dear relative" who had found employment up North. It is also possible, since he evidently sojourned in New York City for some period of time with his wife Henrietta, that while in New York he saw advertisements seeking workers for Vermont-area quarries or factories.

Whatever happened, Williams eagerly made the move. As he wrote, "I FOUND myself enjoying remarkable prosperity among a kind and hospitable people, who in industry, thrift and economy were unsurpassed." Impressed by the possibilities that life in Springfield had to offer, he soon sent for Henrietta and their young children, five in all. At that point they had ten children, but five of them were older and established elsewhere. As he explained:

> The arrival of seven Afro-Americans created some excitement in the little town. I took my family to the Spring Lake Hotel and registered:—Mr. Sam Aleckson, wife and children, South Carolina. The next morning I explained the situation to my employer. He very readily, and with great kindness, placed at our disposal a neatly furnished cottage which he owned.
>
> …
>
> We began housekeeping under very favorable conditions. There was a large apple orchard around the house, and the children were as happy as larks.

Hereafter, Williams's memoir chronicles encounters or mild adventures he experienced with his family during their adjustment as Black South Carolinians to rural New England, and he generally glosses over the challenges they must have faced as outsiders with few connections, much less any racism they may have encountered in what was then and continues to be one of the whitest states in the nation. Very few residents of color were noted in Vermont census records of the late nineteenth and early twentieth centuries.

In Vermont, Williams found domestic work, shoveling snow and maintaining the furnace of an affluent patron. Though this work was difficult, he was now able to provide for his family. He complained about the cold and snow, but also appreciated many aspects of New England life. He especially praised the free and integrated Springfield schools as "perfect." As he saw it, not only did they allowed his children a more consistent education than he had ever received but they were fully integrated and students continued their schooling up through the secondary level. Williams also marveled over the abundance of pie in New England, and describes Springfield as being at "the heart of the pie belt." His joking observations stand in contrast to the poverty and hunger that characterized life for many African Americans left behind in South Carolina during the 1880s and 1890s.

Williams continued to work in the region as a domestic servant for many years, living with his eldest daughter Susan in the households of various wealthy year-long and summer residents of the area. Though the details are uncertain, census data suggest that his second wife died around the turn of the century. By 1910, at the age of fifty-seven, Williams and Susan were both live-in domestics boarding with the wealthy Carter family in Lebanon, New Hampshire, near Springfield. The Carters owned H. W. Carter Clothing, a manufacturing company that began making overalls and evolved into the children's clothing company operating today. While Williams's employment history is a bit murky, he evidently liked the region enough to stay there and see some of his children grow up and find employment of their own. At least one of his sons was listed as a "Porter" working at a Vermont hotel in the 1910 Federal census (Fig. 11).

Williams's interest in education continued long after his own children completed their schooling in New England. Like many former slaves who had achieved their own education only at great cost and with tremendous effort, he was deeply invested in advocating for education for all children, even those who hadn't had the good fortune to attend school in Springfield, Vermont. In the summer of 1915, he penned a letter that was widely reprinted in various Black newspapers around the country concerning a

Barry, Mary	Lodger	F	W	40	S				New Hampshire
Mitchell, Herbert	Lodger	M	W	16	S				New Hampshire
Carter, Augustus H	Head	M	W	48	M1	23			New Hampshire
—, Abbie M	Wife	F	W	41	M1	23	2	2	Massachusetts
—, Marion J	Daughter	F	W	22	S				New Hampshire
—, Donald A	Son	M	W	15	S				New Hampshire
Williams, Susan E	Servant	F	Mu	27	S				South Carolina
Williams, Samuel	Servant	M	Mu	57	M2	12			South Carolina
Thompson, Herbert E	Head	M	W	43	M1	25			New Hampshire

11 Page from 1910 Federal census

SAMUEL WILLIAMS' VIEWS.

Questions Wisdom of Georgia's Proposed Color Line Law For Teachers.

There is much logic in the article of Mr. Samuel Williams of Windsor, Vt., with reference to the attitude of the Georgia legislature toward white teachers in schools for colored people. Mr. Williams says:

I learned through the newspapers recently that a measure had been passed by one branch of the legislature of the state of Georgia barring white teachers from colored schools. For the honor of that state, the nation and the constitution it is to be hoped it will fail to become a law, as it certainly could not be classed as constructive legislation such as the age and the times demand.

After the civil war, when things became somewhat settled, many white ladies in the south, being reduced in circumstances, entered schools that had been established for colored children as teachers. Some had been large slave owners, and their object was not purely mercenary. They desired to repair in part the damage done by the cruel system of which they had formed a part.

They began their labors, it is true, with no very high opinion of the mental capacity of the Negro, but soon learned to love their work, and in many instances showed tender solicitude for those under their care, visit-

ed them in sickness and personally sought the tardy and delinquent.

During my later school years it was my good fortune to have as teachers three ladies of the class to which I refer, and when I was about to leave school it was one of these who grasped my hand and bade me godspeed.

While I remember with deepest gratitude the great benefits I had received in my earlier years from that noble band of men and women of the north who came down to the south, braving abuse from the rabble and ostracism from the thoughtless people of that section, I am glad to offer my humble testimony to the zeal and devotion of those southern white women.

Their mantle may have fallen on others who today even in the state of Georgia may be laboring side by side with the good men and women from the north who are successfully striving to prepare the Negro more fully to discharge the high responsibilities of American citizenship.

Soon this nation may be called upon as the champion of liberty to make good our claim by representing to the world a bold and undivided front, but how shall we do so while 10,000,000 of loyal citizens are ruthlessly and continually discriminated against?

What we need at this time as never before are such measures as tend to harmonize the various elements that enter into the development of that liberty of which Lincoln spoke at Gettysburg.

12 Newspaper article by Samuel Williams, 1915

controversy over what was known as "The Georgia Color Line" (Fig. 12). This legislation sought to restrict Black students solely to Black teachers, part of growing Jim Crow legislation codifying segregation in the United States. Williams argues in his letter for the history of positive relationships between Black and white students and teachers, drawing from his own experiences.

In his letter, Williams tells of the Jones sisters (whom he refers to in his memoir as the "Jaynes" sisters), although in the article he uses neither their real nor their fictional names. He reflects gratefully upon how they, as white women, had defied the norms of culture and caste to teach him to read in antebellum Charleston. He also praises other white women from the South who taught Black children in Charleston during Reconstruction:

> After the civil war, when things became somewhat settled, many white ladies in the south, being reduced in circumstances, entered schools that had been established for colored children as teachers. Some had been large slave owners, and their object was not purely mercenary. They desired to repair in part the damage done by the cruel system of which they had formed a part. ... [their work] showed tender solicitation for those under their care.

Though Williams's experience was being taught to read by white Southern women before the Civil War, after the war white Northern women moved to the South, including to Charleston, to educate Black children. While many of them returned after a few years, the practice of having white teachers for Black students became normalized, if not common. And whether they hailed from the South or the North, they could evidently, as Williams saw it, still make a positive impact upon the students they taught. The type of early twentieth-century legislation Williams discusses in his letter was a bit of a push back against the integration of schools, even if it was integration only of teachers, and this controversy did directly impact Charleston schools. In 1915, the Avery Normal Institute was forced to release all of the white teachers they employed. While this resulted in these white teachers seeking new employment, it also opened up employment opportunities to Black teachers previously not available. In former decades, Charleston legislation placed restrictions on Black teachers by giving white teachers preference for all teaching jobs in the city. As Americans placed sharper focus on segregation, making it illegal for white teachers to work in Black schools, even schools that had a long tradition of interracial teaching were forced to alter their ways, and Charleston's Avery Normal Institute had an all-Black faculty after 1916.

Regardless of the region teachers were from and who benefited from the legislation emerging around 1915, Williams was evidently following this story from afar and keeping up with newspaper reports. He clearly saw the need for the nation to move away from segregation. His letter concludes: "What we need at this time as never before are such measures as tend to harmonize the various elements that enter into the development of that liberty of which Lincoln spoke at Gettysburg."

Long after he ensured his children's education in Vermont and years after penning his thoughts on racially integrated education, Williams moved again to remain near his married daughter in Boston. He appears to have maintained good contact with many of his children and grandchildren, as his descendants today can recall his kindly presence well through the mid-twentieth century. When he passed away in 1946, Williams would have been close to his ninety-fourth birthday.

Cracking the Code

When *Before the War and After the Union* was published in 1929 by Williams's son-in-law and grandson's press, it had the name "Sam Aleckson" proudly affixed to the title page. The book did not make much of a splash in the literary world, and there's no historical evidence that it was reviewed or distributed in any systematic way. It was, nonetheless, evidently treasured by family members and his descendants, and a few precious copies made their way into library collections. Currently, according to WorldCat, there appear to be some twenty-seven extant copies held by libraries and historical societies around the country. The narrative was rarely studied or given much note until 2010 when it was reprinted with the name "Aleckson" in my collection *"I Belong to South Carolina": South Carolina Slave Narratives.*

As noted, like many memoirists, in addition to the pen name "Sam Aleckson," Williams uses a series of false place names and false names for individuals interwoven with actual names of places and people he knew. This poses two problems for his readers: How do we understand his motives, and how do we identify the places and people important to him?

Some of these "code" names are fairly easy to decipher: "Aleckson" is undoubtedly a tribute to his father, Alexander Williams. "Spring Lake,

Connecticut" clearly refers to Springfield, Vermont, a town in Vermont's Connecticut River Valley within the county of Windsor, Vermont (which Williams slyly refers to as "Sorwind" in his narrative).

Other references are harder to identify, yet historical records, such as census reports and city directories, provide significant clues. For example, we can be fairly sure the white women Williams describes teaching him to read, as noted earlier, were the Jones sisters, who, according to the censuses and city directories, lived together on Guignard Street in Charleston at the same time that Williams also reports living there (Fig. 13). Based on an examination of slave schedules—tax documents used to track enslaved property—it also appears likely that one of the Jones sisters owned Williams's father. Other names in his narrative can similarly be identified with some confidence, and many of the names of his own family members can be confirmed through archival documents.

Other details, however, are harder to confirm, and their elusiveness is striking. Most memoirs of experiences of enslavement published after the 1840s faced charges of exaggeration and duplicity, so authors tried to be precise in their details about white people, and forthright in their naming of enslavers. In contrast to Williams's work, such narratives often present more difficulty in tracing the African American family members. Williams instead focuses on providing extensive details and obvious clues about his own family but makes it difficult to trace the white people in his tale. For example, writing in the context of twentieth-century race relations, Williams is careful with his descriptions of influential white slaveholding families in nineteenth-century Charleston. Even several generations after the Civil War, many of these families still held power in Charleston. Members of Williams's own family also continued to live in the city, and some of his descendants still live in South Carolina today. Perhaps for this reason, Williams rarely writes negatively about these prominent white families—the "Bales," the "Deans," and the "Wards"—but he still shies away from directly invoking their true names.

Nevertheless, as I explore in "The People" and the footnotes of this edition, those families are quite possibly branches of the intertwined Deas, Ball or Boyle, and Waring families: all prominent South Carolina clans who collectively owned many dozens of plantation properties and thousands of enslaved people in the Lowcountry region up until

13 Map of Guignard Street, Charleston, South Carolina

the Thirteenth Amendment made the practice illegal. The "Mr. Ward" Williams describes appears to be Joseph Hall Waring II (1823–76), who owned a property known as Pine Hill, likely the "Pine Top" of the memoir. Enslaved people labored at this plantation, which was located along the Ashley River outside of Charleston. And yet, despite all of the description he provides, the names of several of the families and locations Williams cites remain a mystery.

While Williams's code used in his memoir is indeed designed to obscure the identity of individuals, he was sure not to obscure the violence of the slave system he was born into. Williams provided sharp critiques of slavery through descriptions of the sale of children and the violence of beatings. Though Williams did not describe experiencing physical violence himself under slavery, he was conscious of the brutality many others endured.

As with all histories and life stories, Williams's tale is incomplete. His descendants have been able to fill in some details, and archival hunting has uncovered census data, voting records, and other materials; but there is more to know that will add to the complexity of our knowledge of enslaved people's experiences in the United States.

Ultimately, his narrative weaves together a moving story of survival, community, and courageous perseverance. As Williams's title reveals, while slavery was "Before the War," carving out a life "After the Union" also demands recognition. His memoir is a rare account of the Civil War and its Reconstruction aftermath from the perspective of a man who was raised as property but survived to proclaim his own life story as testament to his humanity.

Before the War
and After the Union

Preface

"When I began this unpretentious narrative, I was almost sightless. I had just recovered from a severe attack of illness, during which for a time I became totally blind, and after I was better my eyes seemed hopelessly affected. This I endeavored to conceal as I had to earn my bread, but so frequently did I pass my most intimate friends on the street without the slightest show of recognition that I was forced to admit I was almost blind. I was then urged to consult an eminent physician of the town who gave special attention to ailments of the eye, and after a complete examination, he informed me that my eyes were in such condition that glasses would do me no good, and with a show of sincere sympathy said, "I am sorry for you, but within six months you will be totally blind."

"Approaching blindness is always appalling, especially to one who is dependent on his labor for a living. 'What shall I do when my sight is gone?' This question forced itself upon me night and day. I was then past middle life, and the prospects of a blind and helpless old age stood out before me. My life had not been wholly uneventful; I had been of an observant turn of mind from my youth. What if I could set down the events that had come under my observation in some connected form? Might I not thereby be able to earn something toward my support when I could no longer see!

"I was compelled to give up some of my work on account of failing sight, but I was still employed by day. I began to write at night often under poor light, being scarcely able to see the words as I traced them. Thus my MS. was finished. Untoward conditions prevented publication and it has lain hidden away all these years. The motive that first prompted me to undertake the task no longer exists, my sight has been providentially restored, and at the age of seventy-two I find myself in good health and able to earn my living. There are other considerations, however, which actuate me, even at this late day, to present to the reader this crude story.

"It is a remarkable fact that very many of the immediate descendants of those who passed through the trying ordeal of American slavery know nothing of the hardships through which their fathers came. Some reason may be found in the fact that those fathers hated to harrow the minds of their children by the recital of their cruel experiences of those dark days. There is, however, a deeper reason. It is found in the religious nature of the Negro and the readiness with which he fell under the influence of Christianity, and the zeal with which he strove to follow the teaching and example of the lowly Nazarene.[1]

"If the Negro had emerged from slavery in a sullen and vindictive frame of mind, he would unquestionably have shared the fate of the American Indian, and we would not now be witnessing the marvelous progress he is making, nor his surprising increase in numbers.

"While it is sweet to forgive and forget, there are some things that should never be forgotten. If this humble narrative will serve to cause the youth of my people to take a glance backward, the object of the writer will have been attained. As Frederick Douglass has said, "How can we tell the distance we have come except we note the point from which we started?"[2]

1   A reference to Jesus Christ who, according to the New Testament, grew up in Nazareth.

2   While the origins of this specific quotation are a bit unclear, it appears that Williams is referring to the autobiographies penned by Douglass in which he outlines his early life under slavery to illustrate and frame his path to freedom.

CHAPTER I

Genealogy

"Breathes there a man with soul so dead"[1]

I was born in Charleston, South Carolina in the year 1852.[2] The place of my birth and the conditions under which I was born are matters over which, of course, I had no control. If I had, I should have altered the conditions, but I should not have changed the place; for it is a grand old city, and I have always felt proud of my citizenship. My father and my grandfather were born there, and there they died—my grandfather at the age of seventy-two, my father at seventy-six. My great grandfather came, or rather was brought, from Africa.[3] It is said that he bore the distinguishing marks of royalty on his person and was a fine looking man—fine looking for a Negro I believe is the usual qualification—at least that is what an old lady once told my own father who had inherited the good looks of his grandsire.

1   Scott, *Lay of Last Minstrel*, Canto VI.
2   "Sam Aleckson" is a pseudonym for Samuel Williams, who asserted his copyright in the first edition of this volume in 1929. His father's name was Alexander Williams.
3   "Clement Williams" would have been Williams's great-grandfather's name and, as noted by Williams, Clement was presumably held in bondage by a white family named Williams at some point in time.

I do not know the name my great grandfather bore in Africa, but when he arrived in this country he was given the name Clement, and when he found he needed a surname—something he was not accustomed to in his native land—he borrowed that of the man who bought him. It is a very good name, and as we have held the same for more than a hundred and fifty years, without change or alteration, I think, therefore, we are legally entitled to it.[4] His descendants up to the close of the Civil War, seemed with rare good fortune under the Providence of God, to have escaped many of the more cruel hardships incident to American slavery.

I may be permitted to add that on the arrival of my progenitor in this country he was not allowed to enter into negotiation with the Indians, and thereby acquire a large tract of land. Instead, an axe was placed in his hands and he therefore became in some sort, a pioneer of American civilization.

My father and my mother were both under the "yoke," but were held by different families.[5] They made their home with my father's people who were, of all slave holders, the very best; and it was here that I spent the first years of my life.

My mother went to her work early each morning, and came home after the day's work was done. My brother, older than I, accompanied her, but I being too young to be of practical service, was left to the care of my grandmother—and what a dear old Christian she was![6] At this time her advanced age and past faithful service rendered her required duties light, so that she had ample time to care for me. Her patient endeavor to impress upon my youthful mind the simple principles of a Christian life shall never be forgotten, and I trust her efforts have not been altogether in vain. She was born in the hands of the family where she passed her entire

4   Presumably, the name referenced here is "Williams," the family name that the author and his father are documented to have used.

5   Alexander Williams (?1823–99) and Susan Williams (?1825–95).

6   Samuel Williams's older brother later died during the Civil War while laboring under a Confederate officer. The grandmother mentioned here was, presumably, his father's mother, since at other points Williams explains that he was largely in the care of family members from his father's side. This would have been quite unusual because the ownership of enslaved children would usually be with the owner of the enslaved mother.

life; and it would be a revelation to many of the present day to know to what extent her counsel and advice was sought and heeded by the house-hold—white and black.

Our household was large; beside the owners, three maiden ladies (sisters) there were a dozen servants, some like my father, worked out and paid wages, but all:

> "Claimed kindred here
> And had their claims allowed."[7]

For there never was a better ordered establishment, nor were there ever better examples of Christian womanhood than that of the three ladies who presided over it; and it is especially worthy of note that all the servants who were old enough, could read, and some of them had mastered the three "R's," having been taught by these ladies or their predecessors.[8] Before the beginning of the Civil War these kind ladies liberated all their slaves, and it is no reflection on the Negro that many of the liberated ones refused to leave them.[9] There were many considerations that prompted them to

---

7   The three maiden ladies, the "Jaynes," who helped educate and raise him in his earliest years, were undoubtedly the three Jones sisters of Guignard Street: Elizabeth, Sarah, and Susan. Elizabeth died in 1857, but the other two ladies continued living in Guignard Street during the period Williams depicts. Sarah and Elizabeth Jones are both buried in the cemetery ground of Circular Church of Charleston. One of them may have owned and enslaved Alexander Williams or had some other intricate family connection with the enslavers of Susan or Alexander Williams that evidently allowed for young Samuel Williams to be under their care. The quotation is of unknown origin.

8   The "three Rs" that Williams refers to is the colloquial reference to "reading, writing, and 'rithmetic."

9   It is certainly possible the Jaynes or Jones sisters had liberated slaves at some point and sent them to Liberia, but no documentation has yet been located that thoroughly supports this assertion. As recorded by the 1860 Federal slave schedule, Sarah Jones is listed as owning one man aged thirty-five and Susan Jones is listed as owning one woman aged forty, one man aged thirty-five, one woman aged twenty-five, one boy aged twelve, and one girl aged two. While Williams is clear that he was not enslaved by the Jones sisters, he did spend much of his early years living with them and they evidently enslaved his father, so it seems quite

decline their proffered freedom; in some cases husband and wife were not fellow-servants, and one was unwilling to leave the other. All those who accepted their liberty were sent to Liberia. I know of one who returned after the war to visit relatives and friends. He had been quite successful in his new home, and he gave good account of those who had left Charleston with him. Some had died, others were doing well. He found one of the good ladies still living and had the great pleasure of relating his story to her. When, after a brief stay in the city, he took his departure, he carried with him many tokens of remembrance from their kind benefactress for himself and those at home.

possible that he or possibly his older brother are the young boy listed here as part of their property (even if that was mistaken), and that one of the men listed as owned by either sister could have been Williams's beloved father, Alexander.

CHAPTER II

Childhood

"How dear to my heart are the scenes of my childhood
When fond recollections present them to view."[1]

Though fifty years of time and more than a thousand miles of space separate me from the home of my birth and early childhood, the old home seems more plain before me now than places I visited but yesterday. It was a grand old house, built of grey brick. There were three spacious piazzas running along the west and south sides of the house. The wide yard was paved with brick. To the west of the paved yard was a large garden in which rarest flowers bloomed; but dearer than all to our youthful hearts were the "Four-o'clocks," that grew there in great profusion and various colors. We made festoons of them, hung them over our heads while we "played house" and made mud pies beneath. We wove garlands and twined them about the neck of dear old "Watch." He was our great Newfoundland. Was there ever such a faithful dog as he? Noble animal, rough and tumble with the boys, gentle with the girls, but kind to all. The bulldog and pug have taken his place now, but surely there never was a safer or kinder friend to children than he. Our "Watch" had never

1   Williams appears to be quoting "The Old Oaken Bucket," a poem by Samuel Woodworth, which was set to music by George F. Kiallmark in 1826.

read "The Rights of the Child," but he put his foot, or rather his paw (no small one), down on any of us being punished in his presence.[2] Whenever our parents deemed it incumbent on them to give forcible and painful evidence that they were not amendable to the charge of "sparing the rod and spoiling the child," it was necessary to lock Watch up in the wood-shed, and if in their haste this precaution was neglected he would rush in, seize the slipper or strap (they used both in those days) between his teeth and hang on like grim death. After we had escaped to the yard he would run out, lick our faces and seem to say, "I told you I would not allow it. Come, let us have a romp."

There were fruit trees in our garden; peaches, apricots, pomegranate and figs. We loved the figs most, of which there were several varieties. Our especial pride was the large black fig tree. There were six of us, three girls and three boys. Four of us were white and two were Negroes. Did we quarrel and fight? No indeed! Our little misunderstandings were settled long before we came to blows. There was more of the spirit as well as the letter of the little lines:

> "Let dogs delight
> To bark and bite,"

than seems generally the case now.[3] Would there was more of that spirit abroad in the land today then would we hear less of Negro problems, deportations, and the like.

Every morning in season would find us at our favorite fig tree. The boys would climb into its branches while the girl stood below with extended aprons to catch the fruit as we dropped them. Sometimes there came a voice from above in complaining tones—"Now Jennie![4] I see you eating." "Oh," would be the reply, "That one was all mashed up." "All right, now don't eat till we come down."

2   Williams is referring here to the *Declaration of the Rights of the Child*, penned by Eglantyne Jebb and adopted by the League of Nations in 1924.
3   "Let Dogs Delight to Bark and to Bite" is a poem by Isaac Watts (1715).
4   An enslaved childhood friend.

Then when we descended we took large green fig leaves, placed them in a basket, laid the most perfect fruit thereon, and one of us would run to the house with it. "Don't eat till I come back." "We won't. "When the messenger returned we went to our favorite nook in the garden and after dispatching about a dozen figs apiece we rushed to our breakfast with appetites as unappeased as if we had fasted for a week—And then to school, "But not the Negroes" you say? Yes indeed! The Negroes, too.

The four white children that formed a part of this little band did not live at our house. They were niece and nephew of our good ladies and lived a short distance from us. They came regularly every morning and afternoon, except Sunday, to "play in our yard." They attended a private school, while Jennie and myself, the two Negroes, were taught at home by their aunts for two or three house each day. One of these kind ladies, usually Miss S—,[5] strove with our obtuseness. We had only one book each, but it was a great book. I thought so then and I think so now. From it, like all great men, we first learned our A B C's, then came A-b-âb B-ā, ba and so on to such hard words as ac-com-mo-da-tion, com-pen-sa-tion and the like. From this wonderful book we learned to read, write, and cipher, too. We also got an idea of grammar, of weights and measures, etc. We had slates, for those useful articles had not yet gone out of fashion.[6]

There were pictures in our book illustrating fables that taught good moral lessons, such as that of the man who prayed to Hercules to take his wagon out of the mire; of the two men who stole a piece of meat; of the lazy maids and of the kind-hearted man who took a half frozen serpent into his house. This book was called, "Thomas Dilworth's," and many a slave was severely punished for being found with a copy of it in his hands.[7]

5   This would have been either Sarah or Susan Jones referenced in the first chapter of the memoir.

6   A piece of slate rock surrounded by a wooden frame with a small handle was a common tool to teach writing in eighteenth- and nineteenth-century America.

7   Thomas Dilworth was a Reverend and author of *A New Guide to the English Tongue*. This popular text dated from the 1700s and was revised several times thereafter. It was frequently used in teaching children through the 1800s, although it was relatively outdated by the 1850s. It seems likely it was a book the Jones sisters had held onto from their own youth rather than a new book they would have purchased for an enslaved child's use.

When one had succeeded in mastering the contents of this book (which they frequently did), he was considered a prodigy of learning by his fellows. I do not know whether Mr. Dilworth has ever had a monument erected to his memory, but if ever a man deserved one it is he.

This was a Christian household. The Sabbath was strictly observed. Duties were reduced to the barest necessities, and all attended church. There was no cooking. Cold meats, tea, and bread served to satisfy our hunger on the Lord's Day. The ladies were Congregationalists and attended the "Circular Church."[8] The servants were left to their own choice in religious matters and were divided in their religious opinions. My grandmother was a Methodist and attended "Old Cumberland."[9] It required something very serious to prevent the dear old lady going to prayer meeting on Sunday mornings. These meetings were held an early hour, but I always went with her. Each one entered the sacred place in solemn silence. When the moment arrived some leader would raise one of those grand old hymns such as—

> "Early my God without delay
> I haste to seek thy face."[10]

for they sorely felt the need of him who "Tempereth the wind to the shorn lamb!"[11] Then at the close they sang—

> "My friends I bid you all farewell
> I leave you in God's care

---

8   This church was founded by some of Charleston's earliest settlers as a Protestant church. The building the Jones sisters and young Williams would have known was built in 1804 and burned in 1861, although it has since been rebuilt on the same site of Meeting Street and is now known as the Circular Congregational Church.

9   "Old Cumberland" refers to the earliest Methodist church in Charleston, founded in 1786, which, from the beginning, had both Black and white congregants.

10   The hymn Williams references here is probably "The Morning of the Lord's Day" by Isaac Watts.

11   This seems to reference a proverb which asserts that God will treat those who are weak or unfortunate with greater kindness or mercy than others.

And if I never more see you,
Go on, I'll meet you there."[12]

It not only had reference to the final dissolution, but also to the uncertain temporal condition under which they lived, for, in many instances before the next prayer meeting they were sold, to serve new masters in distant parts. Often without having time to say good-bye to relatives or friends.

When meeting was over they filed out quietly. No buzz of voices we heard until they reached the sidewalk. Then, after a hearty handshake and a word of cheer and hope, they hastened to their duties; many to serve hard and impatient masters. 'Twere well for these that they had been fortified by those few moments of prayer and meditation.

The people showed commendable zeal in attending these meetings. In those early Sunday mornings, men and women might have been seen standing within their gates. They appeared to be listening intently, as if to catch some sound (for they must not be found on the streets after "drum beat" at night or before that hour in the morning).[13] At the first tap they hastened out to their respective places of worship, there to lift up their hearts and voices in prayer and supplication to God.

My mother's people too, were of the "St. Clair" type.[14] On Sundays after Sabbath School I was permitted to visit my mother at their home. They were Mrs. Dane, a widow, and three grown children—a daughter and two sons. The daughter was married.[15] The sons, Thomas and Edward,

---

12   Williams here is likely quoting the hymn "Farewell," by Laurence Sterne.

13   "Dusk Drums" were used in urban Charleston from its earliest settlement years on through the nineteenth century to indicate the curfew for Black inhabitants whether free or enslaved.

14   Williams is here referring to the character of Augustine St. Clare in Harriet Beecher Stowe's novel of 1852, *Uncle Tom's Cabin*. In her novel, St. Clare is a Southern slaveowner who treats the enslaved people under his power with some kindness, although, significantly, he fails to liberate any of them.

15   "Mrs. Dane" was possibly Anna Deas Samuel's mother's enslaver. Anna Deas may have been originally married to a member of the Waring family (hence some of the intricate property and relationships with the Waring or "Ward" family) but remarried into the Deas or "Dane" family. These relationships are a

were unmarried.[16] I always looked forward to these visits with pleasure as I was sure to be regaled with lumps of sugar and pieces of money, by the old lady and the other members of the family. Besides, Mr. Edward (who was a lover of fine horses, and of whom I shall have more to say later), would treat me to a horseback ride around the large lot.

There is nothing good to be said of American Slavery. I know it is sometimes customary to speak of its bright and its dark sides. I am not prepared to admit that it had any bright sides, unless it was the Emancipation Proclamation issued by President Abraham Lincoln. There was often a strong manifestation of sympathy, however. A sad incident which occurred in the Dane family when I was about eight years old may serve to illustrate this: It was usual in those days for each member of a family to have his or her own personal attendant. Mr. Thomas Dane, a kind-hearted gentleman of studious habits and quiet demeanor, had as his servant, a woman called Beck.[17] He did not take breakfast with the family. It was his custom to take his morning meal in his own apartment being waited on by her. Like all the good slaveholders the Danes did not ruthlessly sell their slaves. I do not know how it came about that two of Aunt Beck's children had been sold. She had one remaining child at this time. He was well-liked by all on account of his cheerful disposition. I cannot tell the cause of it, but the boy George was sold away from his mother as had been his brother and sister.[18] This was a heavy blow to her. One morning, shortly after the sale of George, Mr. Dane came down to breakfast. Noticing the dejected appearance of his servant, and no doubt, discerning the cause he ventured some pleasant remark, but Aunt Beck's heart was heavy. At last, no longer able to suppress her great grief she began to weep. "My last chile gone now Mas' Thomas," she said.

bit speculative, but they seem to fit the contours of Williams's narrative and the historical record. If she is the daughter of "Mrs. Dane," as Williams says, that means she was probably Anna Waring Turner, a daughter of Mrs. Dane's (Anna Deas's) first marriage.

16   Thomas was possibly a stepson of Anna Deas or "Mrs. Dane": possibly Edward Waring (not Dane), the son from a first marriage of Anna Deas.

17   Beck would have been a woman enslaved by "Thomas Dane."

18   George was the son of Aunt Beck. He was sold by "Thomas Dane," who was probably a member of the Deas family.

"I know it Beck," he answered, placing his hand to his head, "But, my God! I could not help it."

He rose from the table and paced the floor. The woman became alarmed at the agitation of her master, and forgetting her sorrow for the moment, said, "I know you couldn't help it Mas' Thomas. Sit down and eat your breakfast."

But, no breakfast for him that morning. Presently he went up to his room. Soon he returned having arranged his toilet with more than usual care. He stepped out into the yard, entered an outer building—in a moment a pistol shot was heard! They rushed to the step, but his life blood was ebbing away. He never spoke again. The grief of the woman was more than he could stand.

I visited the place a few years ago. There were different people there. They knew naught of that sad tragedy, nor did they know that Petigrue, Rutledge, Horry, Pringle and Lowndes were once regular visitors here.[19] The old house and its surroundings are very much as they were fifty years ago. The chimes of St. Michael can still be distinctly heard and the hands on the dial may still be seen from the house.[20]

It is quite different at the place where I was born. There is not a vestige of the old house to be seen, for a great fire since that time swept over this district and destroyed it and nearly every nearby dwelling house. In my childhood we had as near neighbors Pinckney, Legare, and Prescott.[21] There is nothing about the locality now to show that here was once the abode of aristocracy and wealth, for, in no instance have the old families

19   The Petigrue (certainly a misspelling of Pettigrews), Rutledge, Horry, Pringle, and Lowndes families he mentions are references to prominent white Charleston families of that era.

20   St. Michael's Church is the oldest church building in Charleston, located on Broad Street and Meeting Street. Its prominent tower would have loomed over the city in Williams's lifetime. Its bells were first installed in 1764 and would have been operational and part of the city soundscape until they were removed during the Civil War.

21   Again, Williams boasts of the prominent associations his enslavers had with the white and wealthy Pinkney, Legare (sometime Legaré), and Prescott families. The fire he mentions is the Great Fire of 1861, which he discusses at length in Chapter XII.

rebuilt their homes here. Very near our house stood a large and quaint old dwelling built before the Revolution. The front door was reached by high flights of steps. I always stood in awe of that house; partly because of the high wall that surrounded it, and partly because once a member of the tribe of "Weary Willies," chanced to pass that way.[22] He sat down on those steps to eat a loaf of bread that had been given him. Whether from hunger or from some other cause (I never knew), he died there with the bread in his hand. As a result, "Go die on Blank's steps" became a phrase of the day.[23] The wall that surrounded that old place was high—higher than any wall appears to me now. It was ornamented on top with glass bottles—broken bottles. The man who broke them seemed to have had murder in his heart. He did not follow any particular line in breaking them, nor did he seem to strive at color effect. There were white, black and brown bottles all broken in a way that was calculated to inflict mortal injury on any who attempted to climb into the enclosure.[24]

But the old house and its high wall too have disappeared. Cotton yards and ware-houses now occupy the site of many an old mansion. Houses have been built on some of the lots, but they are far less pretentious than their predecessors, and are occupied by different people. For—

> "Other men our fields will till
> And other men our places fill
> A hundred years to come."[25]

There were many walls like the one I alluded to in the quaint old city, but they have nearly all disappeared. All the midnight prowler has

---

22 "Weary Willies" was a term for tramps, hobos, or sometimes homeless wanderers or beggars.

23 It appears here that Williams is using "Blank" to avoid naming the actual family that had the homeless man die on their steps.

24 Broken glass is, to this day, not infrequently placed with sharp shards upright into the cement or plaster on the top of courtyard walls in Charleston to discourage intruders or, as Williams also hints, to keep enslaved people in as well. In particular, Williams seems concerned in this passage with chicken thieves.

25 Here the author is quoting an anonymously composed popular song titled, "A Hundred Years to Come."

to do now is to step lightly over artistically trimmed hedges and meander through beautifully laid out walks to the rear of the premises to where the feathery tribe reposes in ornamental structures.[26] But if the glass bottles and high walls are no more, the dim flickering street-lamps have also been replaced by the brilliant electric light, thus enabling the watchful owner to place his "Mustard seed" the more accurately where they would do the most good.[27] Therefore, the "Knight of the feather" may well sigh for the good old "lamp oil" times.[28]

26   Chicken coops.

27   It is not entirely clear what Williams is saying here. He may be making a joke on the biblical parable of the mustard seed, which illustrates a plant that can grow enormously high from the smallest seed. While mustard seed is often seen as a metaphor for faith here it also hints that courtyards can feature plantings that are placed in the most beautiful locations and not simply in locations where they will discourage burglars and help hide chickens. It's a bit puzzling!

28   "Knights of the Feather" suggests a fanciful name for chicken thieves.

CHAPTER III

The Fickle Maiden

"We will ring the chorus
From Atlanta to the sea."[1]

My mother and her children fell to the lot of Edward Dane, brother of Thomas. This young gentleman was of a gay disposition; fond of horses and the sports of the day. Like his brother he was kind and generous. He taught me to ride, and when I could sit my horse well "bare-back" he had a saddle made for me at the then famous "McKinzie's" saddlery, sign of the "White Horse at the corner of Church and Chalmers Street."[2] (Gentlemen had their saddles made to order on those days). I would often accompany him "up the road" on horseback to the Clubhouse, there to exhibit my youthful feats of horsemanship for the

---

1   This is a reference to Henry Clay Work's song of 1865, "Marching to Georgia," which depicted the U.S. Army Major General William Sherman's march to Savannah, Georgia, during the Civil War.

2   See James William Hagy, *Directories for the City of Charleston, South Carolina for the Years 1830–31, 1835–36, 1836, 1837–38, and 1840–41* (Baltimore, Md: Genealogical Publishing Company, 2002), 149. McKinzie's was listed as "McKenzie, A. & R. B., Saddle & Harness Makers, cr. Church & Chalmers. Sts." in the Charleston, South Carolina 1855 *City Directory*.

divertissement of Mr. Dane and his friends.[3] My horse, Agile, and myself were the best of friends. He never hesitated at a hurdle and we never had a mishap. Possibly Mr. Dane had "views" concerning me for he owned several fast horses, but before I was old enough to be of practical service, "Sherman came marching through Georgia."[4]

Here I shall have to admit that I was a "Sherman Cutloose" (this was a term applied in derision by Some of the Negroes who were *free before* the war,—To those who were freed by the war). I am Persuaded however that all the Negroes in the slave belt, And some of the white men too, were "Cutloose" by General Sherman. But let bygones be bygones. "We are brothers all, at least we would be if it were not for the demagogues and the Apostles of hate."[5]

Mr. Edward Dane was an ardent supporter of the "Code."[6] He was an authority in such matters and could arrange a meeting with all the nice attention to details that characterized gentlemen of the "Old School" in South Carolina. His deliberation in such matters would have been a keen disappointment to "Mr. Winkle" as there never was any danger of the police or anyone else interfering when he had matters in hand.[7] The police, however, never interfered with gentlemen of the "Old School" in the "Palmetto" state.[8] The following story is told of a well-known gentleman

---

3   The South Carolina Jockey Club was located north of the city limits at that time and featured a one-mile oval track and clubhouse. The track is still found in Hampton Park in the present-day city limits of Charleston.

4   Williams again seems to be invoking Henry Clay Work's popular song, "Marching to Georgia."

5   Citation is uncertain, but it may possibly be a paraphrase or quotation from South Carolinian Joseph Hayne Rainey (1832–87), the first African American member of the House of Representatives.

6   The "code" here is invoking a cultural understanding of Southern manhood and gentlemanly behavior involving honor, honesty, patriarchal mastery over people within one's control (employees, women, children, and, most of all, enslaved people), and a willingness to resort to violence to defend any slight.

7   In George William MacArthur Reynold's novel of 1864, *Pickwick Abroad; or, The Tour in France*, a character named Mr. Winkle gets into a fight and is rescued by the police.

8   By "Old School," Williams is suggesting that Mr. Dane is known for his traditional style of gentlemanly behavior. South Carolina is sometimes known as "The

of a past generation:—He was a man of splendid physique and dignified carriage. One morning he entered the Old Charleston Market with a lit cigar between his lips. Soon he was accosted by a policeman, a new recruit from the Emerald Isle. "It be aginst the law to be afther schmokin in the Market, Sor," he said. "The law," said Mr. _____. "I am the law. When you see me you see the law. The law was made for poor white men and Negroes." And he strode on leaving that son of Erin a wiser, if not a better man.

The Danes were society people. In their well-appointed home they kept many servants. Mrs. Dane and her daughter Mrs. Turner were both kind ladies. The old lady had a way of personally looking into matters about the establishment that secured for her a pet name from the servants. Whenever she started on her tour of inspection word would be passed along, "de old Jay comin'. This would send every one to their post of duty. Of course the servants were ignorant of the fact that Mrs. Dane knew anything about the re-christening she had secured at their hands. Judge of their surprise therefore, when that lady presented herself before them and announced, "Yes, here comes the 'Old Jay!'"

They were all assembled in the kitchen for a little chat, and their attitudes and the expressions of bewilderment on their faces would have delighted the heart of an artist. The cook was just about to emphasize a remark he had made by bringing a large spoon which he held above his head down on the dresser, when the sudden appearance of the lady and her words, seemed to arrest the descent. There he stood in open-mouthed amazement. Mrs. Dane surveyed the scene for a moment, then quietly withdrew, a smile of amusement on her face. This incident was long remembered by those present, but any reference to it in his presence was promptly frowned down by the Cook, who felt keenly the ludicrousness of the figure he cut with the uplifted spoon. It was as much as their dinner was worth for any one of them even to raise a spoon above their heads.

Uncle Renty, the cook, particularly disliked these periodical intrusions in his domain.[9] The altogether unnecessary clatter and clashing of

---

Palmetto State" because of the many palmetto trees in the South Carolina coastal region.

9   Uncle Renty was enslaved by the "Dane" or Deas family.

pans and kettles whenever the lady made her appearance was only his method of expressing his resentment. This, Mrs. Dane well understood, and never prolonged her stay in the kitchen, for the old man's ability as an artist in his profession was recognized and appreciated. It was said that when the elder Mr. Dane was alive, he frequently began and ended his dinner with one of Uncle Renty's soups. They were simply marvelous, especially his turtle, calf's head and okra soups. How he made them no one knew, nor would they have been any wiser if he had been questioned on the subject. He had several dishes of his own invention to which he had given original names. The other servants had great respect for him; the old, because of his skill, and the young, because of the name of "Old Scarlet" from his fellow-servants. But those who ventured to call him so always took pains to get out of reach. This is how he got the name:—

In those days personal application for work were frequently made from door to door by the "newly arrived." One day an Irish woman applied to Mrs. Dane. She did not need her particularly, but thought she might give the woman work for a day or two as assistant to Uncle Renty, for they were to have a large dinner party:—"Wait a moment," she said. The lady knew the old man well enough to know that diplomacy was required. Going to the kitchen she complimented him on the neat appearance of things. "You are all in readiness for the dinner I see."

"Yes ma'am." (Now the old man had already been apprised of the purport of her visit. He was fully prepared. He was by no means color blind, but was not well posted in the nomenclature of colors.)

"And do you know daddy Renty," continued Mrs. Dane, "I have thought that you might need some additional help in the kitchen for a day or so."

"Everything was all right las time, ain't ee ma'am?"

"Oh yes, certainly. Everything was just splendid," she replied, "But a white woman has applied to me for work and I thought—."

"Mis Charlotte," interrupted Renty, "I don't car if she white as scarlet, ma'am, I doan want um in my kitchen." Argument was useless and so a job had to be found for Bridget in the laundry.

But all of this was before the untimely death of Mr. Thomas Dane, to which I referred in the preceding chapter. That sad event seemed to have been the beginning of trouble for the Dane family. Indeed, things were becoming serious for all. The probability of war between the states was manifested more and more daily. There was a growing feeling of unrest everywhere, and it was soon known that this calamity would not be averted.

The very commencement of the war seemed to have brought disaster to the financial prosperity of many, and the Danes were among the earliest to feel its effects. Some of the servants were sent out to work and so it happened that my mother went as cook for a wealthy family in the city. They were very kind people. Mrs. Bale was a widow with two children.[10] They were both married. Mrs. Ward, the daughter, and her husband lived with her mother.[11] The son, Tom Bale, had establishments of his own.[12]

It was hard for me to leave our dear old home at the Misses Jayne's, my father's people, for there was my good old grandmother, the kind ladies, my playmates and faithful old Watch. But the distance was too far for my mother to walk back and forth (there were no street cars in those days), so we had to make our home at Mrs. Bale's house. I found some consolation however, in our new home. Mrs. Ward had two boys, and they and I soon became good friends. Besides, there were horses there, and Uncle Ben,[13] the coachman, allowed me to ride them to water. There were children living next door too, with whom I became acquainted, and this led to a romantic incident in my life years afterward. When "the Union had come in," I married one of the little girls who lived next door, although I had to go all the way to New York to find her.[14]

10 "Mrs. Bale" was probably a member of the Boyle Family or possibly the Ball Family, both prominent clans in Charleston with many properties in and around the Lowcountry of South Carolina.

11 Mrs. Ward was most likely "Mrs. Waring," who would have been "Mrs. Bale's" daughter (or a Mrs. Boyle's daughter). She and her husband lived with "Mrs. Bale" now and then. Since Joseph Hall Waring II, the likely identity of "Mr. Ward," married a Rosa Wilson Schultz in 1858 and since she was part of a Boyle family and they married at a cousin Mary Boyle's house, we can see that the Waring/Boyle or "Ward"/"Bale" connections are confusing but quite credible.

12 Tom Bale was "Mrs. Bale's" son, and thus possibly a "Tom Boyle."

13 He was the enslaved man who worked as a coachman for the "Wards" (very likely the Waring family).

14 When "the Union had come in" is clearly referring to the post-Civil War Federal occupation of the city. This is one of the only places in his memoir

Our stay at Mrs. Bale's was very pleasant, circumstances being considered. It was here, however that I witnessed the first instance of cruelty or harshness of an owner to his slave that ever came under my personal observation. Of this I shall have more to say. I missed my weekly visits to the Danes too, for besides the pennies, lumps of sugar and horseback rides, I had many friends there also. Then there was Cora, the daughter of one of the servants, I am still inclined to believe that she was the most beautiful girl I have ever seen.[15] She was endowed with an olive complexion, large black dreamy eyes, raven hair, pearly white teeth and a bewitching smile. Her voice was one of the most unusual voices I have ever heard. Cora used to kiss me and call me her little sweetheart (for though you would not believe it now, then I was a bright-looking little tow-headed chap, and got many a kiss from the "big girls" in the neighborhood, because they said I was so cute.) But that was years and years ago. Cora promised to "wait for me." Of course I believed her. She was eighteen and I was about nine years old, yet I thought that somewhere in the race of life I would overtake her and she would be mine. It never occurred to me that when I had reached eighteen she would be twenty-seven, and the disparity in our ages would be the same. Years afterward I met her. She was married and had several children, while I was just entering into young manhood. How fickle some girls are, eh?

where he reveals anything about who was probably his second, not his first, wife. According to the 1880 Federal census, Williams was married to Mary Artson, a seamstress. She appears to have died in the early or mid-1880s. By 1888, evidence suggests that Williams had remarried a woman (possibly called Henrietta) who is most likely the wife he mentions here as moving to Vermont with him. In the 1910 Federal census it is noted that Williams is on a second marriage and has been married for twelve years in that second marriage although he was not living with this second wife in 1910. At that point he was living with his daughter Susan and working as a servant to a Vermont family. Perhaps the marriage failed, and his second wife left him. It is hard to know. The name "Henrietta" has its origins in some lost document of unknown attribution, so it is mentioned here only as a possibility. Williams may have had older children with Mary Artson and younger children or stepchildren with Henrietta who could have made up the ten children he reports in this memoir.

15   Cora appears to have been the daughter of one of the enslaved laborers held by the "Bale" or Boyle family.

There was a large garden with fig trees and flowers in it at Mrs. Bale's house, but the figs were not as sweet nor were the flowers half as beautiful as those at my old home. There were two dogs not near so clever as our Watch, and the children—well, they had never lived at a home like our old place on Guignard Street. In fact, there never was another home like that, but "Grief sits light on youthful hearts."[16] All my regrets were greatly modified by the prospects of a visit to the country. Such a trip always seems alluring to a city boy. Indeed, the country seems to hold out allurements to everyone except those who live there. Mr. Ward owned a plantation to which the family went every winter, and when it became known to me that we were soon to go there, I was all impatience.[17] I plied Uncle Ben with a thousand questions as to how far away it was, what kind of a place, what was to be seen, were there any snakes, did they bite, was there any wild horse running about in the woods, did he think I might catch one? Etc., etc. Now Uncle Ben was a philosopher. He was not given over much to talking. No one but myself would have dared to ask him so many questions. He had taken a fancy to me. Everyone said it was a wonder. He had no children of his own, besides he was inclined to be somewhat of a misanthropist. I would sometimes have to wait indefinitely for an answer to a very simple question. However, by the exercise of patience and discretion I finally got all the information I desired, or thought I did, which amounted to the same thing.

Uncle Ben was epigrammatic as well as philosophical. One night after a very trying day he went to prayer meeting. He was feeling rather blue, and did not intend to take an active part in the exercises. Of course the conductor of the meeting knew nothing of the old man's frame of mind. "Will brudder Ben jine us in prayer?" he asked, but there was no response.

16   This phrase may have just been a common saying, but it has no known origin I can identify.
17   "Mr. Ward" can be identified with near certainty as Joseph Hall Waring II (1823–76), a large slaveholder with extensive family connections throughout South Carolina. He served in Company K, 4th South Carolina Cavalry, which was sent to Virginia during the Civil War. He was a State Senator in 1865. He owned Pine Hill and Clayfield plantation labor camps in Dorchester County, South Carolina, just north of Charleston. Pine Hill would thus be what Williams refers to as "Pine Top."

"I mean brudder Ben Bale," he said, fearing there might be some misunderstanding. Being thus importuned the old man knelt down and delivered himself as follows:—"A ha'd bone to chaw. A bitter pill to swoller." Bress de Lawd. Amen.

But Christmas was approaching, and Santa Claus was gleefully expected for the good old man was a real personage in those days—not a myth. Oh, but you say it was wrong to deceive the children, as it had a bad effect on them? I don't know, but it seems to me that the children who believed in Santa Claus in those days would at least compare favorably in their love of truth with those of the present day who know, "It is only father and mother." At all events the country was forgotten for a while. It was sometime after holidays that we left for the plantation. There was not a gayer boy than myself when we boarded the train. (This was in the year 1860).

When we arrived at the station there were three teams awaiting us; one for the family, one for the servants, and another for the baggage. Uncle Ben was there, having brought the horses up by road a few days before. I rode on the baggage wagon. As there were only the driver and myself on it I thought I could ply the former for information without being requested to "Hold my tongue," an operation that I had always found difficult. My companion I found was a well grown boy whose name was Missouri. Why they gave him this name I do not know. Perhaps it was in honor of the "Missouri Compromise." He said his name was the same as that of a great country miles and miles away, that he was called "Zury" for short, that his principal work on the plantation was plowing, and that his mule, Jack, was the best plow animal on the place. He also informed me that there were a large number of children on the plantation whose work was to play, and to keep the rice birds out of the fields. I suppose he was thoroughly dry by the time we got to "Pine Top," but he was a good-natured fellow. We became firm friends. I always rode his mule from the field to the barn. Zury is now living in Charleston, where he is a successful mechanic known as Mr. Ladson.[18]

Anyone visiting the old time plantation must have been impressed by the boundless hospitality of the people. Everybody came to see us. They

18   A Zury Ladson is listed as a "colored" laborer residing at 12½ Glebe Street in the *Charleston, South Carolina, City Directory*, 1881.

brought chickens, eggs, potatoes, pumpkins, plums, and other things too numerous to mention. I soon found many play fellows. My especial chums were Joe and Hector, sons of the plantation driver.[19] The boys were somewhat older than myself. They were skilled in woodcraft, and taught me how to make bird traps and soon had me out hunting. One morning early, we started out, taking their dog, Spot, along. When we reached the woods the dog ran ahead briskly, barking as he went. Shortly he began to bark furiously. "Spot, tree," said Joe, and we hastened on. When we got to the dog he was standing by a tall stump, still barking. "Got er rabbit," said Hector.

"Where?" I inquired.

"En de holler," he replied, and thrusting his arm into it he drew out the poor trembling creature by his hind legs.

"Set him down!" I cried.

"Oh no," said he, "Ee might git 'way."

This was just what I wanted, for I pitied the little animal, but the boys were hunters. They were not going to risk losing their game, so they killed the frightened thing without further ceremony, and put him in their bag. We got three rabbits that morning. I did not enjoy the sport, nor did I partake of the rabbit stew they had for dinner. I did enjoy the night hunts however, for coon and possum were our quarry. I went with some of the young men. While the harmless little rabbit will not even defend himself when attacked, the possum is shy and crafty and the coon will fight. One night the dogs tree'd a coon. Now the wily animal usually selects a tree from which he can reach another, but this coon did not have time to "pick and choose." There was no other tree within jumping distance, so he went out on a limb as far away from the body of the tree as possible. And there he sat. As it was a large tree, it was decided that instead of cutting it down, someone should go up and shake the game off of it. Sandy, one of the party, readily volunteered to do so. Reaching the limb on which the coon was "roosting," he went on it so as to give it a vigorous shaking. The limb broke and down came both man and coon. The coon was dispatched while some of the men went to the assistance of Sandy. We thought he was

19 Joe and Hector would likely also have been enslaved by the "Ward" or Waring family.

seriously injured. He was stunned for a moment, but as they raised him up he asked, "Did we git um, boys?" The fall of more than twenty feet was broken by the branches beneath him, and thus he soon was all right again.

These hunts were great, but they were nothing compared to the feasts that followed. These were never held on the same night as the hunt, but on the one following. I never took kindly to either the coon or the possum. The former is usually too fat, and the habits of the other do not appeal to me. But the stories told at these feasts! They would make the fortune of a writer if he could reproduce them. They simply cannot be reproduced, that is all. To get the real, genuine, simon pure article, one must be on the ground.[20] And perhaps you think that you have heard good, sound, hearty unadulterated laughter. Well, may be.

You may disfranchise the Negro, you may oppress him, you may deport him, but unless you destroy the disposition to laugh in his nature you can do him no permanent injury. All unconscious to himself, perhaps. It is not solely the meaningless expression of "vacant mind," nor is it simply a ray—It is the beaming light of hope—of faith. God has blessed him thus. He sees light where others see only the blackness of night.

---

20   By the mid-nineteenth century, the phrase "Simon Pure" suggests absolute and untainted purity. Its origins, which would likely have been unknown to Williams, are from a reference to a character named Simon Pure in a play of 1718 by Susannah Centlivre titled *A Bold Stroke for a Wife*.

CHAPTER IV

The Lover

"The tide of true love never did run smooth."[1]

PINE TOP, Mr. Ward's country seat, was a beautiful plantation about eighteen or twenty miles from Charleston.[2] The house, an old colonial mansion, stood on elevated ground, well back from the main road, and commanded a fine view of the surrounding country. From the main road the house was reached through a wide avenue, lined on either side by giant live oaks, while immediately in front of the house was a large lawn circled by a wide driveway.

From the front door of the house the barns, stables, gin-house, corn mill and Negro quarters, presented the appearance of a thriving little village. The quarters were regularly laid out in streets, and the cabins were all whitewashed. I once read in a newspaper, a letter from a Northern man who visited the South immediately after the war. He took a rather unfavorable view of the prospects of the Negro, for he said, "There was a

---

1   Here Williams misquotes Lysander's line in Shakespeare's *A Midsummer Night's Dream*, Act 1, scene 1: "The course of true love never did run smooth."
2   "Pine Top" plantation labor camp was almost certainly Pine Hill plantation labor camp, alongside the Ashley River, and in Dorchester County, slightly north of Charleston and southwest of Summerville, South Carolina.

lamentable absence of flowers about their cabins." I suppose this "Oscar Wilde" thought the conditions under which the people had lived were well calculated to foster love of the beautiful.[3] The poor fellow could not have visited Pine Top however, and many other places I could name, or he would have been delighted to see the well-kept little flower beds near many of the cabins. And no doubt, he would have said they were just "too, too" for words.[4] He might even have been tempted to enter some of those cabins by their neat and tidy appearances which could be seen through the open doors.

Mr. Ward was what was called a "good master." His people were well-fed, well-housed and not over-worked. There were certain inflexible rules however, governing his plantation of which he allowed not the slightest infraction, for he had his place for the Negro. Of course the Negro could not stand erect in it, but the Negro had no right to stand erect. His place for the Negro was in subjugation and servitude to the white man. That is, to Mr. Ward and his class, for while he maintain that the supremacy of all white men over the Negro was indisputable, and must be recognized, still there was a class of white men that he would have prevented from ever becoming slaveholders.

While I repudiate Mr. Ward's views I am bound to believe that there is something in blood. In those parts of the South where aristocratic influence is dominant, opposition to the advancement and progress of the Negro is far less than where the contrary is true. Eliminating the Negro altogether, in some of the southern states the "bottom rail" has gotten on top with a vengeance, and where such is the case, it is very bad for the "enclosure."[5]

3   By invoking here the poet and playwright Oscar Wilde, Williams suggests the observer of the cabins is excessively obsessed with the role of the beautiful over other concerns.
4   In this passage, "too, too" implies the position of a person impressed beyond the point of words (perhaps affectedly so) with the conditions of the flower beds. While this phrase was not one directly associated with Wilde, it would have been in keeping with the tone expressed by a dandyish aesthete for the purposes of this imagined scenario.
5   Williams is arguing that the least-cultured and least-educated class of ungentlemanly white men are in power in many areas of the South.

One evening Mr. Ward sat in his library before a blazing wood fire. He was the picture of contentment; and why should he be otherwise? He had a beautiful wife, two fine boys, hundreds of acres of land and numerous slaves to work them. Furthermore, he had just dined on wild duck. Now I would not tax the credulity of the reader by an exact statement as to how long those ducks had been allowed to hang up after being shot before they were considered "ripe," but, they had reached a stage that would hardly have been appreciated by a man of less "refined" taste than his, for Mr. Ward was a lover of "high game."[6] The aroma that arose from those "birds" during their preparation for the table would not have tempted the appetite of an ordinary man, even if he were very hungry.

Mrs. Ward had joined her husband for a little chat when Jake, the waiting boy, entered.—(Jake was the assistant and understudy of Uncle Sempie, the veteran butler. Uncle Sempie always retired after dinner, leaving Jake to attend to the later wants of his master.)[7] "Mingo, fum Mr. Hudson place wan ter see yo, sah," he said.[8]

"All right, let him in," said Mr. Ward.

Presently Jake returned ushering in a very young Negro who appeared to be laboring under some embarrassment. As he entered he said, "Ebenin sah, ebenin ma'am."

---

6   Williams is trying to explain that "Mr. Ward" (or Mr. Waring) liked strong-smelling, almost rancid, meat—"high game" would be meat in early stages of decomposition.

7   Jake was another young, enslaved person at the "Pine Top" labor camp and Uncle Sempie was an older enslaved man who served as a butler to the "Ward" family.

8   Mingo was man enslaved at another local plantation labor camp within walking distance of "Pine Top." He visited to spend time with Dolly, the woman he later marries. The fact that he is not owned by "Mr. Ward" and yet at a later point in this narrative "Mr. Ward" directs him to be whipped goes unremarked in this memoir but is a notable demonstration of the absolute power white enslavers had over Black people regardless of the chain of ownership. A Black man named Moses Hudson shows us in the 1880 Federal census as living in Kershaw, South Carolina (not far from the area where the "Pine Top" property would have been) with a wife, Millie, and a young boy named Mingo Hudson. It seems possible that Millie might be "Dolly" and Moses could have been "Mingo" in the narrative. As Williams notes, a Mr. Hudson was Mingo's enslaver.

"Good evening," replied the lady and gentleman.

"Are you Mingo from Mr. Hudson?" asked Mr. Ward.

"Yees, sah."

"How are your master and mistress?"

"Dey berry well, sah."

"Well, Mingo, what can I do for you?"

The young fellow hesitated as if he did not know exactly how to proceed. Both the lady and gentleman looked at him attentively. He was becomingly attired, had a pleasant face and was evidently a favored servant. At last he mustered enough courage to say, "I come sah ter ax yo p'mission ter cum see Dolly. Dolly is the darter ob Uncle Josh and Ant Peggy, sah," he added.[9]

Mr. and Mrs. Ward strove hard to suppress their mirth as they saw the poor fellow was about to collapse. "Oh," said the lady smiling, "So you would a-courting go, eh?"

"Yees, ma'am," recovering himself a little.

Mr. Ward cleared his throat. "Well Mingo," he asked, "Have you got your master's consent?"

"Oh yees sah."

"And you and Dolly understand each other?"

"Yes, sah,"

"Are Josh and Peggy willing to have you for a son-in-law?"

"Oh yees, sah. I don ax dem."

"I suppose you behave yourself. I am very particular concerning this matter."

"I know dat, suh. Mas Jeem kin tell yo about me, sah."

"Well, I guess it is all right. Of course I shall inquire about you. Have you got your ticket?"[10]

---

9   The father and mother of Dolly continued to serve "Mrs. Ward" (or Mrs. Waring) after the war. Dolly is the daughter of Josh and Peggy. She later became the wife of Mingo. See the previous note about her possible identity.

10   It is likely that Williams is referring to what is known as a "slave pass." A slave pass was a written document that showed that the slave was allowed to leave their master's property. Any slaves found without a pass could be arrested, fined, or detained as a runaway.

Here Mingo produced the desired article. Mr. Ward read it, his brows contracting a little. "This is all right," he said, returning the paper, "Except that it does not say where you are to go. Now I never allow anyone on my place with such a ticket. The next time you visit Dolly you must have a different 'ticket.' Ask your master to give you one stating plainly that you are to visit my plantation. Do you understand?"

"Yees, sah."

"Well Mingo, I wish you good luck!" said Mrs. Ward.

"Tankee ma'am, tankee sah," and he bowed himself off.

The "ticket" referred to was simply a permit showing that the slave had his or her master's consent to be absent from home. In some instances their destination was mentioned; in others it merely stated that "A— has my permission to be absent on such a date, or between given dates." Mr. Ward never refused his people "leave of absence," but in every case their destination was clearly set forth. It would not be safe for them to be found "off the coast."[11]

Now I would not insinuate that Mingo was a fickle lover. It is just possible that he wished to visit some of the other girls in the neighborhood simply for the purpose of convincing himself by actual comparison of the superior charms of his own Dolly. His was a monthly "ticket," and under these circumstances we must excuse him for not wishing to have it changed. In fact he determined not to do so. He did not even acquaint Dolly with Mr. Ward's instruction. Possibly he feared that she might have agreed with that gentlemen—from different motives of course.

It was the custom of the owner of "Pine Top" during his stay on the plantation to visit the "Quarters," ostensibly to see how his people were getting on, and incidentally, to note that things were as they should be on the place.[12] Mingo was aware of this so he thought that on his future visits to his sweetheart all he had to do was "to lay low" until Mr. Ward had made his rounds. In this he was successful for a time but—

11   "Off the coast" means off the plantation or the agreed-upon routes to the declared destination.

12   "Quarters"—buildings or areas where enslaved people were expected to live.

"The best laid plans of mice and men, gang aft agley."[13]

Besides, young love is ever impatient.

One night he took his stand in his usual place of concealment. It had been raining and the weather was decidedly cold. He had waited long after the usual time for the gentlemen's visits. "Spec de old feller ain't comin out tonight," he said to himself.

Mingo did not know Mr. Ward. The people on Pine Top expected their master at any hour, and were not surprised to have him present himself at their doors when *he* thought they were not looking for him. He would sometimes even partake of roast possum or coon. Unaware of these habits Mingo hastened to meet the warm welcome that awaited him at Dolly's cabin. He was destined to receive a warmer welcome than the one he anticipated.

Uncle Josh and Aunt Peggy sat by the fire. *Perhaps* they were asleep. Dolly and Mingo were sitting at a small table as far away from the old folks as they possibly could get. "I bin ober to Cedar Hill las nite," he began, "An I see'd the new-gal dey got. I tink she is—."

"I see'd her," interrupted Dolly, "An I tink she's just horred."

And Mingo deeming discretion the better part of valor said, "I tink so too."

Just then there was a loud rap on the door and Mr. Ward entered! Sometimes the very means we use to conceal our fears serve but to make them plain. The moment Mingo sighted Mr. Ward he became alarmed, but he must appear collected.

"Ebenin sah. Cole nite, sah. How is Missus and de chillum?"

Immediately Mr. Ward knew "the lay of the land." "Oh they are all well. How are all at Laurel Grove?" he asked smoothly.[14]

---

13 This quotation is a reference to Robert Burns's poem, "To a Mouse." The original text reads: "The best laid schemes o' Mice an' Men / Gang aft agley, / An' lea'e us nought but grief an' pain, / For promis'd joy!" "Gang aft agley" is Scottish dialect, probably meaning, "often go awry."

14 "Laurel Grove" was evidently the plantation labor camp where Mingo was enslaved. As with the names of many sites Williams mentions, this could be a number of other sites where groups of people labored in bondage within walking distance of "Pine Top." It might be in the location of North Charleston today

"Berry well, sah, all berry well."

Mr. Ward turned to speak to the old people, taking good care to place himself between Mingo and the door. When he started to leave the house he seemed to remember something. "Oh, by the way Mingo, did you have your ticket changed?"

"Mas Jeems, he bin gon ter town, sah, an Miss Liza say wait til he cum back."

"Ah, then you had it changed when he came back, did you?" Mr. Ward spoke very deliberately.

"When he git back I so busy I forgot, but I hab um fix sho fore I cum er gen, sah."

It was a cool night, but there were signs of perspiration on Mingo's face as he spoke. "I am afraid to trust your memory, Mingo," he said. Then he stepped to the door placing the silver mounted cow's horn which he always carried about the plantation, to his lips, blowing a loud blast.[15]

The Driver

Uncle Joe, as he was called by the Negroes, and Daddy Joe as he was called by the white folks, was Mr. Ward's driver.[16] He was a plantation Negro, the son of a plantation Negro, but he would not have answered to any of the descriptions usually given to the "plantation Negro." He did not have a receding forehead, a protruding jaw, nor bandy legs. In fact, he bore a striking resemblance to a well formed man. He had a thoughtful expression, and although he was rarely seen to smile, he had a pleasant countenance. He was not harsh with those over whom he had been placed. "Boy, doan lemme put me han on yo," was sufficient to bring the most refractory into line, and this was not a mere figure of speech, for when his

occupied by a Laurel Grove subdivision neighborhood. Of course, Williams might have been using a fictional name for this plantation labor camp as he did with other locations.

15   "Mr. Ward" or Mr. Waring here blows the horn to call Uncle Joe to punish or torture Mingo for "forgetting" to update his slave pass.

16   Uncle Joe or "Daddy Joe" was "Mr. Ward's" or Mr. Waring's driver or overseer.

hand did drop on the shoulder of some erring culprit it came down with a force; the effects of which was felt for a long time after, for he was a man of unusual strength.

But Uncle Joe could laugh, and when he was engaged in relating some particularly ludicrous adventure of Brer Rabbit and Brer Wolf, to his two boys Joe and Hector, at night when the day's work was done, his sonorous voice could be heard throughout the Quarters.[17]

This night the old man had removed the tension from the boys' minds by completing a Jack O'Lantern story begun on the night before.[18] The story was as follows:

"Wonce der was er man. He lib on won plantation en his wife an chillun dey lib on er noder, seben mile off. Von nite de man tink he go see dem, so he ketch er fat 'possum. He put de possum en some oder tings een er bag en start. Wen he git good way on de road he see er brite light. (Dem Jack O'Lantin always lookin out fur trabblers). De lite blin de man an he los de road. Fus ting he kno he fine de man heself een a swamp. Den de jack O'Lantin laf en say, "Now I hab dat bag." De lite gon out wuick en de man cudent see he han befo he face."

Here the old man pleaded weariness and sent the boys to bed, promising to finish the story the next night, for though Uncle Joe had never written a continued story he understood the art of creating a demand for the next number. All the following day the boys talked about the probable fate of the luckless traveler. "I bet," said Joe, "Dat Jack Lantin tak de man bag, den kill um."

"He doan hab ter kill um he self. All he hab ter do es to tak way he bag en lebe um een de dak, en sum ob dem bad wile varmint wat be een de swomp eat um up," answered Hector.

17   Uncle Joe would have been telling folktales about animal trickster figures, the kind of tales that were later made famous when reframed and retold by the white author Joel Chandler Harris.

18   This tale is likely a version of an Irish folktale that had been known and repurposed into African American oral storytelling traditions. Indeed, in 1935, Zora Neale Hurston collected one such story in her collection *Mules and Men* (Philadelphia: J.B. Lippincott Co.) about a jack-o'-lantern trying to entice and trap a slave.

But to their great relief their father had skillfully extricated the poor fellow from his perilous position, bag and all, with no greater misfortune than the loss of his hat which was brushed off by the low hanging branches. His shoes came off in the soft mud of the place. These he did not stop to hunt for as he was glad to get out alive. The boys, thus satisfied went willingly to bed, while Uncle Joe settled himself for a quick nod by the fire. Aunt Binah, his wife, busied herself cleaning up supper dishes.[19] As she went about her work she hummed an old plantation hymn; the humming grew louder as she continued, and soon she began to sing—"I run from Pharo, lem me go."[20]

This seemed to arouse her husband, for he commenced to beat time with his foot. When she reached the chorus he joined in and their strong voices blended harmoniously.

> "De hebben bells er ringin, I kno de road
> De hebben bells er ringin, I kno de road
> De hebben bells er ringin, I kno de road,
> King Jesus sittin by de watah side."

"Hush," said Aunt Binah, "Tink I yer de hon." They both listened attentively. Yes, there was another blast. "Wonder wha dat debble wan wid me now," said Uncle Joe. He slipped on his shoes, got his hat and coat, (meanwhile his wife had lighted his lantern), and hurried out. As he stepped outside a third blast assailed his ears; this to direct him, as Mr. Ward had seen the light.

"Um soun like he ober to Josh house. Wonder wha da him now?" he said to himself, hastening along.

"Ah Joe," said Mr. Ward as the driver reached Josh's cabin, "Mingo has forgotten my orders. Take him over to the barn and give him twenty lashes."

"Cum on boy," said Uncle Joe, not unkindly, yet in a tone that indicated there was to be no hanging back. Under these circumstances Mingo

---

19   Uncle Joe's wife.

20   While it is not entirely clear, the lyric here and the ones that follow may be a variation of the spiritual best known as "Go Down, Moses."

must be excused for not having lingered to say "Good night." In fact, "his heart was too full for utterance."[21] And so the line of march was taken up in silence, Uncle Joe leading with his lantern, Mingo next, Mr. Ward bringing up the rear. When the humiliating performance was over, the party broke up. Mr. Ward returned to the house whistling softly:—

"From Greenland's icy mountains."[22]

Uncle Joe, wending his way back to his cabin, sang in a low voice, "There's rest for the weary."[23]

Poor Mingo neither sang nor whistled. As he painfully took the shortest cut for the main road he conso'ed himself with the thought that— "Faint heart never won fair lady."[24] He did not put it just in that way. What he really did say to himself was, "Well, sum time man hab ter go tru heap to git wife."

Did he win his Dolly finally? We shall see.

21   The phrase here is aptly taken from the words of poet James S. Gibbons, which were set to a music and became a popular song of the Civil War era, known as "We Are Coming Father Abraham." This song was used to recruit and celebrate the mission of the Union troops. For Mingo it invokes his sorrow and fear that pushes him beyond words. The original lyrics of the opening of one of the best-know versions ran:

> We are coming, Father Abraham, three hundred thousand more,
> From Mississippi's winding stream and from New England's shore.
> We leave our plows and workshops, our wives and children dear,
> With hearts too full for utterance, with but a silent tear.
> We dare not look behind us but steadfastly before.
> We are coming, Father Abraham, three hundred thousand more!

22   "From Greenland's Icy Mountains" was a popular hymn composed by Bishop Reginald Heber in 1819.

23   This could have been paraphrased from any number of hymns or spirituals, but the point here is that Uncle Joe seems to have some sympathy for Mingo and is expressing it in song.

24   A common proverb.

CHAPTER V

The Hunting Season at Pine Top

"The Old Flag never touched the ground."[1]

The Color Sergeant[2] at Battery Wagner

Gay hunting parties composed of friends from the city and ladies and gentlemen from the surrounding plantations often assembled at Pine Top. Many amusing tales were told there of the "Stag Fright"[3] and blunders of amateur sportsmen on their first deer hunt. There was a Mr. Brabham, a carpenter, who being placed at a "stand" for the first time, and told not to let the deer pass him, waited in breathless anxiety.[4] Soon a magnificent buck came bounding towards him almost within arms' reach. Throwing

---

1   Williams here cites a song published in 1901 celebrating the heroic actions of a member of the famous Black 54th Massachusetts Volunteer Infantry and Medal of Honor recipient, Sergeant William H. Carney at the Battle of Fort (or Battery) Wagner. The song, "Boys the Old Flag Never Touched the Ground," was written by Bob Cole, James Weldon Johnson, and J. Rosamond Johnson for their Broadway musical "Shoo Fly Regiment."

2   "Color Sergeant" denotes the soldier whose responsibility is to carry the flag or colors.

3   This is most likely a play on the term "stage fright."

4   A carpenter and friend of the "Ward" or Waring family who was included in their hunting party event.

up his arms wildly, his gun held aloft, he exclaimed, "I wish I had my hatchet!" while the terrified animal sped on to be brought down by a more collected hunter on the next stand.

This year however, the festivities were cut short, for Mr. Ward was often called to the city as indeed were many of the other gentlemen who were accustomed to join the gay throng at Pine Top. It was soon known that they were attending Mass Meetings and Conventions.[5] Sometimes Mr. Ward would be absent several days. There were strange whisperings among the Negroes. "Dat ting comin," they said mysteriously to each other, "Pray my brudder, pray my sister." I listened with wonderment, but was taught to say nothing.

Uncle August was Mr. Ward's right hand man.[6] He was equally at home in the fields or in the house, and could always be depended on in an emergency. He was full of humor, a born mimic, and could set those about him in gales of laughter, without seeming to try. Mrs. Ward frequently conversed with him when he was engaged in some task under her directions about the house, or grounds. One day while he was moving some pieces of furniture from one room to another the lady said, "Daddy August, do you know there is going to be war?"

"War! ma'am, Wey, ma'am." Anyone who saw and heard the old man would have been ready to affirm most positively that this was the very first intimation he had had of the impending conflict.

His mistress certainly thought so.

"Why here," she replied.

"On dis plantation, ma'am?"

"Oh no, I don't mean that exactly, but you see, the Yankees are determined to take our Negroes from us, and we are equally determined that they shall never, never do so. Why Daddy August, don't we treat you all well?"

"Ob cose yo does, ma'am. Wha dey bodder deyself bout we fer?"

---

5   This appears to be a reference to the South Carolina Convention of December 20, 1860, a meeting in which the decision for South Carolina to secede from the Union was made.
6   Daddy August was an enslaved man who worked closely with both Mr. and Mrs. "Ward."

"That's just it; they are simply jealous to see us getting along so well, and they want to take our Negroes and put them at all kinds of hard work, like horses and mules. They are sending emissaries among our Negroes to make them dissatisfied.

"Wha dem is, Miss Em'ly?" (Of course he had not the slightest idea what an emissary was!)

"Oh they are men who will try to sneak around and talk to the Negroes."

"Wha dey gwine say?"

"Well, they will tell the Negroes that they are their best friends, and so on, just for the purpose of deceiving them you know."

For a second there was a twinkle in Uncle August's eyes which Mrs. Ward did not observe. "Mis Em'ly," he asked with a startled expression on his face, "Wha dem embassary look lak."

"Oh they will be in disguise, you know, but they try to look like our own people. Why?"

"Well yo kno, toder day wen I bin gon ober ter Mr. Hudsin, ma'am? Wen I coming back an git mos to de big gate, I see er strange man comin' up de road. Time as I see um I tink bout dem "Kidnabber" cause you kno dey car off Mr. Hudsin Tom."

"Now Daddy August," interrupted Mrs. Ward, "I don't believe any kidnapper carried off that boy. I think he just ran away."

"Wha he hab ter run away fer, Mis Em'ly? I sho Mr. Hudsin es er good man!"

The aforementioned Tom was at this very moment on the way to freedom by means of the "Underground Railroad," and this Uncle August knew very well.[7]

"Enyhow I fraid dem kidnabber so I mak hase git inside de gate. Wen he git ter de gate he call ter me "Cum yer. I wanter tell you somting."

I say, "Cum een, sah."

---

7   While there may have been certain individuals in South Carolina who could have assisted fugitives in some situations, there was no organized "Underground Railroad" or activist, abolitionist community in South Carolina during this era. By the early twentieth century, when Williams wrote his memoir, the "Underground Railroad" was often invoked as a loose term and indicating here simply that Tom had escaped.

He say, "No, yo cum yer."

I say, "I see Mas Henry cummin an I ain't ga time. (You kno Mas' Henry gon ter town dat day). Time as I say dat he hurry way."

"I see yo ergan," he say. Den I say ter maself I know dat da "kidnabber."

"Did you see him again?" asked Mrs. Ward quietly, but she did not succeed in hiding her alarm from the old man. He knew what effect his story (and it was a great big one), would have.

"No, ma'am!" he answered, "An I doan wanter see um gan noder."

Mrs. Ward was determined to acquaint her husband with what she had heard, as soon as possible. Therefore, when Mr. Ward returned from the city that evening, she informed him privately of what August had told her. He was even more disturbed than she was. "And," she added, "Daddy August is frightened half to death."

They both concluded that the stranger was a Yankee spy. "It will not be good for him if I find him prowling about here," said Mr. Ward, "I shall question August further about it."

He found an opportunity that evening, without appearing to attach any importance to the incident, to question the old man closely. However, August had nothing to add to what he had told Mrs. Ward. He considered it was already a sufficient "whopper."

But Mr. Ward was uneasy. He told Uncle Joe to have two horses saddled, and they rode over to Mr. Hudson's. He did not acquaint the driver of the object of the visit, but that was not necessary as August and Joe had already had a hearty laugh over the hoax. From Mr. Hudson's they went to Mr. Benton's.[8] To each of these gentlemen Mr. Ward related what he had heard. Neither of them had seen or heard of any stranger in the neighborhood. They both promised to look out, and if such was found it would not be their fault if he did not account of himself. But the mysterious man was never found of course.

Some days after the incident just related Mrs. Ward was superintending some work which Uncle August was doing in the garden; setting out plants and the like, for it was now early spring. A team drove up to the house and the men proceeded to unload a tall pole. "Wha dey gwine do out dey, Mis Em'ly?" asked the old man innocently.

---

8   A neighbor of "Mr. Ward."

"Why they are going to set up a flagpole. You see we are to have a government of our own so we must have a flag of our own; the Confederate flag. It is going to be a very pretty one, too."

"No priteer dan de old flags upstars."[9]

"Oh yes, a great deal prettier," but the lady was thinking of the old flag her father and grandfather had fought under.

The old man glanced at her. "Well," said he, "It hab ter be berry puty ter beat de old flag." There was more in his words than he meant his mistress to understand.

"Daddy August," said Mrs. Ward, as though not wishing to speak anymore about flags, "We will put that right here," (alluding to a plant the old man held in his hands).

August did as directed, but he was not quite through yet. Presently he said, "Mis Em'ly, wha yo gwine do wid de old flag? Yo pa and yo granpa use ter tink er heap ob dat one."

"Burn it up!" replied Mrs. Ward in rather a vehement tone.

Uncle August knew he had said enough.

It was now about the middle of April 1861. Important matters seemed to require Mr. Ward's attention in the city, and much of his time was spent there. One evening Mrs. Ward told Uncle Ben he must meet Mr. Ward at the station the following day with a pair of horses. He usually used a single horse and a dog cart for this purpose. "Sumting up," said the old coachman to himself.

Mr. Ward had not been home for near two weeks. The Negroes on the plantation knew war was approaching, for though they could not read the newspapers, it is remarkable how well posted they were in regard to the trend of events. They knew also that their master's long absence was to be accounted for in the coming conflict. His return therefore, was anxiously awaited by them; as they hoped to gain some information as to how matters actually stood.

The next morning Uncle Ben had his team in tip top shape, and himself rigged up with his regulation coachman's outfit, including his shiny silk

---

9   The traditional American Flag with horizontal stripes and a blue corner of stars is evidently what Uncle August is disingenuously remarking upon.

hat. He carried Jake along to open the gates. "I kno wha he want," he had said, "But wait little bit." And he drove away.

As they left the station Mr. Ward said, "Save your horses Ben," but when they swung into the plantation avenue he told the coachman to "let them go."

Uncle Ben pulled up his lines, drew the whip lightly across his horses and said, "Git out."

Tom and Jerry responded and they came up the "home stretch" in fine style.[10] The whole family stood on the front porch waving their hand-kerchiefs. Mr. Ward waved his in return. As Uncle Ben drew up at the stepping stone, Mr. Ward sprang out, ran up the steps, embraced his wife and children, and kissed his mother-in-law, (a thing which I believe men seldom do). "We have taken the fort," he said, and they entered the house.[11]

10   We can presume here that Tom and Jerry were the names of a pair of horses being run fast to dramatize the impressive entrance Mr. Ward was determined to make.

11   As explained in the passage that follows, on April 11, 1861, Fort Sumter, which is off the coast of Charleston, was attacked by the Confederate army, and Major Anderson, the Union commander in charge of the fort, was ordered to withdraw. He refused, and the Civil War is generally understood to have begun at that moment.

CHAPTER VI

The Beginning of the End

That night conflicting emotions governed those who lived on "Pine Top" plantation. In the big house there was gladness and rejoicing, while at the Quarters there was groaning and lamentation. The Negro believed that as long as Major Anderson held Fort Sumter their prospects were at least hopeful; but when Sumter fell, they felt that their hopes were all in vain. Though the future looked dark, there were two on the place who never gave up; Uncle Ben and Aunt Lucy.[1] You are acquainted with the old man already. Aunt Lucy was the plantation nurse. Years of hard and faithful toil in the fields had gained for her respite from active labor. It was her sole duty now to take care of the young children of the women who had to go into the rice and cotton fields, and those mothers were glad indeed to have such a kind Christian woman as she was to look after their little ones while they were at work. The old woman, though well on in years, was still hale and hearty. "Min, wha I tell yo. De Master gwine bring we out," were her words of encouragement to those who were ready to despair. Uncle Ben's words were, "Dem buckrakin laf now, but wait tel bime by."[2]

---

1   Aunt Lucy worked as a nurse.
2   According to the *Oxford English Dictionary*, the word "buckra" was an African American term referring to white men.

Between the "big house" and the Quarters there was a spring from which the people got their drinking water.[3] Every afternoon a long line of children might have been seen with "piggins" on their heads, taking in the supply for the night.[4] On the evening of Mr. Ward's return, the children did not appear. In their stead, and at a later hour, their parents came. It was noticeable too, that they lingered at the spring, being concealed from view by the trees that grew about it. The reason of all this was that arrangement had been made with Jake that as soon as possible after dinner, he was to run down and tell them any news he might gather during that meal. Jake, as a possible gatherer of news! Why that was absurd! He was spry enough about the house and dining-room, but otherwise he was as dense as a block of stone. At least, that was what his master would have said of him. This density on the part of the Negro was, in fact, a weapon of defense—the only one he had. Do you think Captain Small could have run the Planter out of Charleston harbor if it was thought he had sense enough to do so?[5] No, indeed! He never would have had the chance.

I said Jake was to run down. That was a mistake. He was much too wise for that. After dinner was over he sauntered down the back steps as soon as he could. Upon reaching the ground, he thrust his hands into his pockets, and walked slowly toward the spring, whistling, "Way Down Upon the Swanee River," as though he didn't have an idea in his head.[6] "He comin' now," said Aunt Lucy, "Well mi son, wha he say," as the boy drew near.

"Well, ma'am, dey tak de fote. We done now," was heard on all sides.

3   The "big house" would mean the domestic space inhabited by the White family and, sometimes, the enslaved people they used for domestic service. "The Quarters" would be the housing area allocated to most of the other men, women, and children forced to work on the property.

4   "Piggins" are small pails or buckets.

5   "Smalls" was Robert Smalls, an enslaved boatman who escaped using a Confederate ship called the Planter. He later became a Union Navy captain, businessman, and politician.

6   He is singing a line from "Old Folks at Home," a minstrel song written by Stephen Foster in 1851.

"Wait, chilun, hope pray," was the old woman's encouraging words as she proceeded to question the boy further. "Wha dey do wid Majer Ande'son?"[7]

"Dey le him go."

"Wha dey say bout him?"

"O he say de Majer es er brave man. He mak er speech befo he cum out. He say, (and Jake drew himself up to imitate the Major) "Genlemen, if I had food fer my men, an ambunachun I be dam if I wud le yo cum en dose gates!"

"Amen, bress de Lawd!" cried the old woman.

"O Aunt Lucy!" said Manda, the housemaid, abashed at the old woman's endorsement of the somewhat impious remarks of the gallant Major.[8]

"Hole yo tong yo braze piece. Go on Jake mi son."

But the boy had little more to tell and so the people went sadly back to their cabins. Aunt Lucy's parting words were, "Hope chilun, pray chilun."

The next day Mr. Ward gave Uncle Sempie orders to prepare for a large dinner party that would be given by him in a few days. This was to be another addition to the long list of similar functions that had taken place at Pine Top under the supervision of the old butler. Among them there was one to which the old man often referred with special pride. It was the great dinner given by Mrs. Ward's grandfather, (for Pine Top had been the home of the Bale's for generations) in honor of the Hon. John C. Calhoun.[9]

When the day for Mr. Ward's great dinner came, the guests began to arrive early; some on horseback, others in carriages, the coachmen vying with each other in the style in which they came up the avenue, and pulled

7   Major Anderson was a Union officer who held Fort Sumter during the beginning of the Civil War and was forced to surrender the federal fort to the Confederate forces in order to save the men under his command.

8   Manda: an enslaved housemaid.

9   The prominent statesman from South Carolina, John C. Calhoun, who served as a Congressman, Senator, Secretary of War, and Vice-President, among other positions. He died in 1850. Thus, this prestigious social event mentioned by Williams must have occurred in at least a decade or more from when he heard about it and thus it must have loomed large in the memories of the Pine Top community for them still to be making references to it through the early 1860s.

up at the stepping stone. There were distinguished ladies and gentlemen. There were horses that had records, and some of the coachmen had records, too. York, Mr. Boyleston's coachman, was one of these.[10] His horses always showed the best of care and his stables were models of neatness and appointment. He had three well grown stable boys under him who were kept at rubbing and polishing constantly. The boys slept at the stable while York occupied a neat little cabin on a hill a short distance away. Seen early in the mornings coming down to look after his stock, with a cigar in his mouth, he might easily have been taken for Mr. Boyleston himself. As he neared the stable he would say, "Ahem!" and each boy popped his head out and would say, "Sah." Upon entering he went through a minute inspection, and it was for their best interest if everything was found in perfect order. York had the record of having once knocked his master down.

The circumstances which led to this daring performance were these: Mr. Boyleston took great pride in his horses. His stock was always of the finest strain, and it may be added that he appreciated his coachman's ability as a whip and manager. His special pride was a span of dark gray trotters of undoubted pedigree. For these he had bought an expensive pair of blankets. "Now, York," he had said, "These blankets have cost me a great deal of money. Be very careful with them. Never allow the horses to wear them at night."

York took as much pride in those beautiful coverings for his horses as did his master. He never permitted the boys to touch them, but each morning after the finishing touches to the animals, he adjusted them with his own hands. One morning he led the horses out on to the floor of the barn, hitched them, and threw the blankets lightly over them, while he took another horse outside to water. Unfortunately he had tied the animals too closely together. They began biting at each other as horses are wont to do. One of them got his teeth into the blanket of the other, pulled it down on the floor, and together they trampled it under hoofs. The boys were at work at a distant part of the place therefore could not see what was

10 York was "Mr. Boyleston's" enslaved coachman. Many people named Boyleston lived in the Lowcountry region of South Carolina, but it is possible that this was Henry Boyleston, an enslaver based in Charleston, who, according to the 1860 Federal slave schedule, held nineteen slaves.

going on. When York returned he was dismayed at the sight. The once beautiful blanket now stained and torn, lay under the feet of the horses! He picked it up, but there was nothing he could do to repair the damage. He placed it on the horse as best he could. To add to his confusion he saw Mr. Boyleston coming down to the stables for his usual morning inspection. The coachman walked to the further end of the barn, pretending to be engaged at some work, while his heart beat almost loud enough to be heard.

"York," called out Mr. Boyleston as soon as he entered and his eyes fell on the damaged blanket, "Did I not tell you never to let the horses wear their blankets at night?"

"I dident, sah, de—."

"You are a—liar, sir—."

Out flew York's right arm before he knew it, and down went his master. He walked out into the lot, folded his arms, and stood facing the door. Mr. Boyleston got up. As he came to the door York said, "Shoot me down, sah." His master drew his revolver. "Fire, sah, I'se ready," and York stood unflinchingly.

Mr. Boyleston put up his pistol. "Come here to me, York," he said.

"No, sah."

"May I come to you?"

"Yees, sah! I wudent ham a hair on yo head."

"York," said Mr. Boyleston walking out to his coachman, "How came that blanket to be in such a condition?"

York gave his master a straight account of the whole occurrence. "Here is my hand; I was wrong," was Mr. Boyleston's magnanimous answer, "Do not mention this to anyone."

There were not many masters like this one.

Mr. Ward's dinner was a grand affair, and no one rejoiced at its success more than old Uncle Sempie. After dinner the party went out on the lawn where a stand had been erected. Amid cheers the new flag was raised and many gentlemen made speeches which all seemed to be aimed at the "White House."[11] I did not know where that was, but Uncle Ben said it was

---

11   "The White House" here is used as a synecdoche for the entire Federal government, which was led at that time by President Abraham Lincoln.

where "dem buckra wud nebah git."[12] Later I learned that the White House was at Washington, and sure enough they never got there.

Mr. Ward now deemed it necessary to have the plantation carefully guarded at night. For this purpose he chose two young Negroes, brothers, Titus and Pompey.[13] The confidence the southern white had in the Negro, and the fidelity of the latter to the trust reposed in them speaks volumes. Here was this master perfectly satisfied to place the safety of himself and family in the hands of these men, on whom, at that moment, he was seeking to rivet the chains of slavery forever. The men were to relieve each other, and at stated intervals, if things were all right, they were to come under Mr. Ward's window and sing out, "All is well!" If things were otherwise, they were to pull a knob which would ring a bell in their master's room.

Titus was noted for his prodigious strength, and an equally enormous appetite. He created great amusement one night during his watch by standing under the window and shouting, "All is well and I'se hungry!" Mr. Ward took the hint and thereafter the men were each provided with a large "hoe cake," lined with fat bacon every night before going on duty.

The time drew near for our return to the city. We must not remain on the plantation after the tenth of May, for those not acclimated are liable to contract malarial fever.[14] Soon we bid farewell to the old place and to the many kind friends we had met there. The kind-hearted people loaded us with simple gifts. My stay in the country had been most pleasant.

12   While in previous passages of this memoir "bukra" is used to reference all white people, in this instance it is being used more precisely to indicate white Southern or Confederate forces that, as Uncle Ben predicts, will not succeed in winning the war by taking the White House.

13   Two enslaved men under control of "Mr. Ward."

14   Malaria, a parasitic infection spread by mosquitoes, and endemic to South Carolina, particularly in the Lowcountry swamps and planting areas, was a notorious killer. Seeking to flee the disease, many wealthy planters and their families would seasonally leave the region.

CHAPTER VII

In Town Again

"Mischief, thou art afoot."[1]

O n arriving in Charleston we found great excitement there. Men were going about the streets wearing blue cockades on the lapels of their coats.[2] These were the "minute men," and the refrain was frequently heard,

> "Blue cockade and rusty gun
> We'll make those Yankees run like fun."[3]

Soldiers on parade often passed by our house, and we ran to see them. One day a troop of horses went by. The ladies waved their handkerchiefs and the officers saluted. I heard they were on their way to the "Front." I

---

1   From Shakespeare's *Julius Caesar*, Act 3, scene 2.

2   A "cockade" would be a knot of ribbons used as a kind of badge.

3   Minute Men were members of secessionist militia groups that were often absorbed into the Confederate Army as a whole as time went on. The phrase was deliberately used to invoke terms used for soldiers of the American Revolution. These lines were from a song commonly sung on the streets of Charleston as was reported by various contemporary witnesses and reporters of that era.

wanted very much to know where that was, therefore, when Uncle Ben and I went to the stable I asked, "Uncle Ben, where's the 'Front?'"

The old man made me no immediate reply. In fact, he never did. Knowing he heard me I waited patiently. Presently he looked up:—"De front, boy, es de place weh dem young buckra gwine ketch de debble," he said, and resumed his work.

Mr. Ward had received a commission in the army with headquarters at Secessionville.[4] It chanced that Mr. Edward Dane was appointed on his staff, and he took my brother, several years older than myself, into the army with him. But the dear boy contracted fever and soon died. Later, the command was removed to another point in the harbor, and for a short time I took my brother's place as officer's boy! And here I must admit I wore the "gray."[5] I have never attended any of the Confederate reunions. I suppose they overlooked my name on the army roll! I carried a knapsack, too. My uniform consisted of a confederate gray jacket, blue pants, and a Beauregard cap.[6] My knapsack was somewhat smaller than the regulation article, and was covered with glazed leather. It usually contained clothes going to or from the washerwoman in the city. I had a day in the city every week and thus had ample time to do my shopping which usually consisted of five molasses groundnut cakes, at one dollar each![7] They were not quite as large as those you get for a penny now, either. Once I went to buy a pair of shoes and the storekeeper charged me seventy dollars for them. I tried several other stores and finally got a pair for sixty-five dollars.[8] Talk about little things being high now, why then most things were literally "out of sight"—especially things to eat.

4   "Secessionville" is an informal name for a small army encampment on James Island, South Carolina.
5   The grey uniform associated with the Confederate rebels.
6   This outfit would have been similar to the clothes allocated to actual low-ranking Confederate soldiers.
7   Molasses and groundnut (peanut) cakes were a popular treat sold on the streets throughout the city of Charleston.
8   It is difficult to know exactly what kind of banknotes or currency he was working with, but his examples illustrate the wartime scarcity, rampant inflation, and deprivation of wartime Charleston.

In the early part of our day on the Island things were reasonably plentiful.[9] The real business of the struggle had not yet begun, and General Ward still had cattle at Pine Top. It was his custom to occasionally have a lamb or a "Harry Dick" dressed on the plantation and shipped down to the Island.[10] On these he regaled himself and brother officers. And, "Hereby hangs a tale," from which we get another glimpse of the general's limitation for the Negro.[11]

General Ward had a boat's crew of six men. With one exception they were detailed soldiers—up country men—who had little knowledge of the management of boats. The exception was Dick Brown, a Negro fisherman.[12] As is well known the fishermen in and around Charleston have no superiors in the handling of small craft on the river, or in the open sea. Dick pulled the stroke oar, acted as coach, and when the wind was fair, he sailed the boat. Relying on Dick's skill and knowledge the general had never missed a trip on account of weather. On one occasion he presented his crew with a side of meat and they appointed one of their number who had had some experience as a butcher, to cut up and share it. The general chanced to pass by while the sharing was in progress. "Ah boys," said he, "Sharing up?"

"Yes sir," replied the butcher, "There are six of us and I am trying to divide as equally as possible."

"Oh well now, I certainly want Dick to have a portion, but I did not expect him to share equally with you white men; a Negro must never share equally with a white man, you know." Where was Dick while this was going on? He stood among the speakers together with Jake, the general's boy and I, for Mr. Ward would never think of being so "unjust" to a Negro as to speak behind his back.

---

9   When Williams talks about "the island," he is most likely still referring to James Island off the coast of South Carolina near Charleston.

10   This is method of preparing meat specific to this era.

11   This is likely a reference to Shakespeare's *As You Like It*, Act 2, scene 7, l. 28. The original phrase, "thereby hangs a tale" essentially means "there's a story behind this."

12   Dick Brown: A knowledgeable fisherman skilled in the Lowcountry waterways.

There are two of us alive today. I don't know where General Ward is, but I do know that he is dead. Shot did sometimes fall thick and fast on the Island, but *then*, the general, had the benefit of the sea breeze!

The command was soon ordered to Virginia, and I, being too young to be taken along, was given an indefinite furlough.[13]

During the latter part of my stay on the Island things were tight. As for provisions, well, there weren't any to speak of. Ground-seed corn and hominy with an occasional piece of bacon, was considered very acceptable.[14] Those advocates of "plain food" should have been with us. Nothing could have been more plain than our fare. I don't believe it was unhealthy either, although I have had no desire to try it again. "Pie" is good enough for me.[15] For coffee we had parched grist steeped and sweetened with molasses, "Mule Blood" brand.[16] I went over from the Island in Mr. Ward's boat every Saturday. There were steamers that ran regularly to our Island, ("The Planter," of heroic memory was one of these), but they only crossed at night so as to avoid "salutes" from the blockading fleet.[17] Most of the officers of our command kept row boats in which they could reach the city at their pleasure. Our landing place at first was Market Dock, but when General Gilmore began to raise the temperature in the lower part of the city, we moved our moorings further uptown; for it would have been rather unpleasant to be standing on a wharf and have a shell come

13   Williams is invoking military language here with a "furlough," but he is simply indicating that he was sent back to the Charleston property under the control of the Ward and Bale families (again, that was likely referencing the Waring and Boyle families).

14   Hominy is made from ground corn and can be used for grits or cooked into a mash of sorts.

15   Why he sets apart the word "pie" here in quotation marks is unclear, but pie becomes a recurring theme in his later chapters concerning his life in the north and the bounty of food he found there.

16   Parched grist would consist of corn kernels roasted and often ground up. The term "Mule Blood" is associated with a specific type of dark molasses.

17   *Planter* was the name of the boat commandeered by Robert Smalls so that he could escape with his family to the Union forces. Here he means the steamers would need to avoid getting shot at by the Federal boats trying to enforce a blockade on Charleston.

whistling by taking one's head off.[18] Furthermore, the head might roll overboard, or else the kind comrade who picked it up might, in his haste, be apt to clap it on again upside down, or backside front; and like the lady who did not receive an invitation to the "pink tea," one would never feel the same again.[19]

"The Old Coffee" and "DeKalb" belonged to our fleet.[20] Captain Christian of the "Coffee" was one of the most popular seamen at the port of Charleston—"as jolly an old sea dog as ever drank grog."[21] I always returned to the Island at night by steamer. Several times, random shots fell near us but we were never hit, and soon got used to them. When one came skipping toward us we simply said, "Shoo fly." At this time I was about ten years old, and rather small for my age. I shall never forget the peals of laughter that greeted my first appearance at headquarters. I boarded the Old Coffee at "Market Dock" and was met on the other side by Mr. Dane who took me up to the place. Then I was taken into a large room in which were General Ward, Captain Parker, Lieutenant Tompson and Jenks.[22] "What in thunder are you going to do with that boy!" they cried in unison.

"This boy is all right Jim," said Mr. Dane looking at Lieutenant Tompson, "He can ride." The laugh was now turned on the lieutenant who, as I afterwards learned, had been thrown from his horse a few days before.

---

18   General Quincy Adams Gilmore, a Union general during the Civil War who was involved in the Union recapture of Fort Sumter.

19   Williams is likely referring to what was known as a "pink tea," an event for women and by women where they would gather and discuss women's suffrage. It was called "pink tea" and was disguised by frilly, feminine décor to keep men from attending.

20   The *Coffee* and the *DeKalb* were steamships used for missions in the Charleston harbor.

21   This is presumably a quotation from a popular song. Captain Christian remains hard to identify.

22   Lieutenant Tompson was probably Hugh Smith Thompson, who went on to become the governor of South Carolina. Captain Parker was likely William Harwar Parker (1826–96), who was an officer first with the United States Navy but later with the Confederate States Navy. General Ward is the probable pseudonym of a member of the Waring family as discussed in the list of "The People" found at the beginning of this edition. The identity of Jenks is unclear.

My duties were very light. If any of the old soldiers are now living who were on that Island at that time, (1862–63), remember seeing an officer splendidly mounted, followed by a mite of a Negro boy also mounted, galloping over the Island, the boy was myself. Those who remained at home in the South had many privations to bear, of which I got my full share. Things that we consider common necessities now, were luxuries then. The people who sometimes clamor for war have no conception of what it really is. But let us not dwell on these harrowing times of the past. May we never see the likes again!

CHAPTER VIII

A Turkey Stew

Turkeys and even chickens were very scarce on our Island. It is remarkable how quickly these creatures disappear from the neighborhood of a soldier's camp during war times, especially when rations are scant. I suppose they become alarmed and fly away. Some people may be of a contrary opinion, but we will let that pass.

Adjoining our Quarters there lived an Irishman who owned some turkeys. Besides these there was not so much as a turkey feather for miles around. At this time one of these festive birds was worth his weight in gold. But, there was not gold in circulation hence the amount of confederate money it would have taken to buy one would have equaled the turkey himself—at least in bulk. When Mr. O'Flanagan wanted to buy a piece of real estate, or make some similar investment, he just sold one of his turkeys to some young officer who was willing to part with a small fortune. For these and other reasons you may be sure that Pat kept watchful eyes on his flock.

One afternoon one of these turkeys, without the fear of consequences, flew over into our yard. We had a dog that would "fetch," therefore, Jake quietly remarked, "Sic um, Bull." In less than no time Bull had that turkey by the neck, and in equally short order, Jake had that bird in a bag.

The fence between the lots was a high one. Those on the other side could not see what was going on in our yard, but they heard the dog chasing the turkey. Therefore, it was not long before Mr. O'Flanagan presented himself to the sentinel at the gate. "I wud loike to go in an git me turkey," he said.

Now the soldier had seen what was going on, and with visions of a midnight roast before him, had become a party to the transaction. With a view of allowing Jake time to "cover his tracks" he resorted to "dilatory" measures.[1] "What kind of a turkey was it," He asked with an innocent look on his face, and when he could think of no other questions to ask he told the man he would have to see one of the officers. "There is General Ward coming up the street now," he said, and Pat hastened to meet the general.

"Yr haner, one av me turkeys flyed over de fince an oi belave some wan was afther sittin the dorg on im."

We have already seen that General Ward was a strict disciplinarian even in civil life. He was no less so as a military man therefore he told the Irishman to go in and look for his property, and if he found that any damage had been done to it, he should have ample satisfaction, as he never allowed any crooked proceeding about his headquarters.

In Pat went. He searched in all the out-buildings, high and low without success. He went to the kitchen where Jake was busy getting the general's supper. "The Giaral sa'd oi cud luk fer me turkey. De dorg—"

"Dog nebbah bring no tukey een yer," said Jake, "Yo ken look, doe."

But the search revealed no trace of the missing bird and Mr. Patrick O'Flanagan left muttering "imprecations not loud but deep."[2]

Does the devil take care of his own? I don't know, but during the hunt in the kitchen Jake's heart was in his mouth, for the turkey was hanging peacefully in a bag behind the door where he might easily have been seen if Pat had only looked there.

I do not know whatever became of it. It was never cooked in that kitchen. Jake became alarmed and took it away under cover of night.

Many a story is told about the camp fire, and many a dainty bite goes round that never came from the commissary.

---

1   Delaying measures or acts to slow down the hunt for the missing turkey.
2   Williams is paraphrasing Shakespeare's Macbeth here: "curses, not loud but deep" (*Macbeth*, Act 5, scene 3).

CHAPTER IX

Tom Bale

"If thine enemy hunger, feed him."[1]

In a previous chapter I promised to say something further about Mr. Tom Bale. It was his habit to spend a week or more with his mother every year, and during our stay at Mrs. Bale's, and after our return from Pine Top he made one of his yearly visits, bringing his wife and child, nurse, coachman, and three horses.

It is said that no man is wholly bad. If this is true why the young man of whom we are going to speak must have had his redeeming qualities. But they were never manifested in the treatment of his slaves. He was a very young man. His father had died when the son had barely reached his majority, and he was left in sole control of the large plantation on which were more than four hundred Negroes. It was said, he had from his youth exhibited an ugly disposition, and this early elevation to power did not tend to improve his character. In many instances where the master was harsh, the mistress was considerate; while in others the reverse was true. In either of these cases the servants had a chance, but where both were alike inconsiderate, the fate of the slave was hard indeed ... . Young Mrs. Bale was hard to please.

1   From Romans 12:20.

Some say that even the devil is not as black as he is painted. I never could endorse that statement. I have always thought he was as black as it was possible to paint him, and a great deal blacker. At any rate I am free to say there was not one, single, mitigating feature in the treatment of those unfortunate creatures who had to serve Tom Bale; they all suffered. A doubled share seemed to fall to the lot of "London," the coachman.[2] To say that this poor fellow had a hard time would convey but a faint idea of his condition. He was competent, faithful and submissive, but these qualities did not secure for him the slightest consideration. Frequently, after going over the cushions, etc., with her handkerchief, his mistress would send the carriage back to the stable as being "Absolutely too dusty to ride in." The slightest complaint from Mrs. Bale exasperated his master against him and he was often severely punished even though he had done all in his power to have everything in perfect order. His patient fortitude under cruel treatment was indeed wonderful. Despite the terrible hardships he had to endure, he managed to extract some pleasure from his occupation. He loved his horses and often spoke of them in terms of endearment. "Dem boys nebber mak me shame yit," he would say in speaking of them, "Wen I say cum Dandy, cum Spug, de Negger dat pick me up got ter know ha be bout."

London and I were the best of friends, and so as to be on hand each morning when he went to the stable I was permitted to occupy a cot in his room, for I liked to go with him. He went much earlier than Uncle Ben. The poor fellow was glad to have me with him at night. It was a relief to him to have someone to talk to. He would tell me about the fine horses he had handled, and others he had known: Of Old Tar River, Bonnet so Blue and Clara Fisher. When he was seated on his box flourishing his whip with the easy grace of the experienced southern coachman, one would not think his life was the terrible grind it really was.

One morning at a very early hour I heard Tom Bale calling from the yard, "London, London!" I tried to rouse the sleeping man without success. Presently I heard the heavy tread of his master coming upstairs.— And London slept!—The balmy air of that spring morning was seductive.

---

2   London was an enslaved coachman working for "Mr. Bale" or probably a Mr. Boyle.

The night had been rather warm and London was not encumbered with any superfluous clothing. Now London was very careful with his whips. They were not allowed to lay about carelessly, but were suspended from a rack of polished wood, made for the purpose, and hung against the wall in his room. There was one gold mounted, one mounted with silver, and one was adorned with carved ivory, one had a dainty little red ribbon bow on it, while the two others were decorated respectively with white and yellow.

Bale pushed open the door and strode into the room. He looked at the sleeping coachman a moment, then, with a muttered imprecation, took down one of those whips; I don't know which. I heard the "swish" through the air, for by that time I had covered my head. London thus rudely awakened sprang from the bed. Blow after blow descended upon him until the blood started. "Now," said the tyrant fairly exhausted, "Go down and hitch up my horse! I told you to have my buggy ready early this morning." The abused and bleeding Negro hastened to obey.

Tom Bale had intended that morning to drive up alone to one of his plantations twenty miles from the city. He had hitched a fast young horse to a light buggy. The mistreated London who had handled this animal from a colt had once ventured to warn his master about driving him with an open bridle. In truth, he tried to prevent Bale from possibly having his neck broken. That b—d—, the bully had replied, "I want his head to show. He has the finest head in South Carolina."

But that morning it appears retributive justice was at his heels, for, late that afternoon the horse reached the plantation with a part of the harness clinging to him; clearly evident a runaway. As you probably know this created no small stir in the place. A searching party was sent out immediately. "Here Ceasar, you take Sancho and two or three other. Hasten out, take lanterns with you. I will follow with a team," and Jim Black, the overseer, hurried away to the barn.[3]

It was remarkable how much time Ceasar managed to consume in getting ready though apparently using all possible expedition. At last they were off. "Cum on boys," he said as they got out into the main road and he stared on a brisk run in the direction in which it was least likely to find

---

3   Jim Black: He was an overseer who might have been a free white man or could have been an enslaved man assigned to a position of authority.

the missing man. They had gone nearly a quarter of a mile before Black drove out. He yelled at them to come back. Their confusion was so very evident that he simply abused them roundly as a pack of blockheads, and sent them down the road toward the city.

They hunted some miles before any trace of Tom Bale was discovered. At last they found a piece of leather—some part of the harness. It was now quite dark. Lanterns and torches were lighted. A little further on they came to a place where the vehicle had evidently left the road. A few hundred yards out in the pine woods the upset buggy was seen, and nearby lay the young man, pale and unconscious. Even Ceasar felt pity for him.

He was lifted into the wagon in which the overseer had thoughtfully placed a small mattress. He had also dispatched a messenger on horseback who met them on their way back. Upon a hasty examination the physician found that Bale had one leg broken and his shoulders severely bruised. It was weeks before he could be removed to the city, and months after the accident before he was able to get about.

This summary visitation of Providence, should, it would seem, have cured this rash young man; but it did not. At this time the war is on and Tom Bale is impatiently awaiting his physician's permission to join his regiment at the front. The newspapers are giving glowing accounts of Confederate victories. The white people are exultingly jubilant, and the Negroes correspondingly sad and depressed, for though they cannot read the newspapers they are well posted as to the news that comes in.

One morning Mr. Thomas Bale was seated on his piazza in Charleston, reading. The reports of Confederate success pleased him. London, with his heart bowed down was sweeping the sidewalk in front of the house when a fellow sufferer passing by stopped to exchange the usual morning greeting.—"Mornin' brudder Lon'on."

"Mornin' mi brudder."

"How yo gittin on?"

"O mi brudder, ha'd time, an wus cumin," was London's sad reply.

Out flew his master, and with the heavy cane he had carried since his accident he felled the poor slave to the earth. "Say better times are coming, you rascal," he stormed, re-entering the house.

And what did this much abused Negro do? The war being over Tom Bale returned to his home broken in health and fortune; for despite his injured leg he had gone into the war and remained until the end came. At this time many of the men who were engaged in the southern side during the war, not knowing what would be their fate under the new order of things, were hastening out of the country. Bale was among these. He was forced to leave his family inadequately provided for. However, he was still a young man and hoped to retrieve his fortune in a foreign land, or at least to remain away until things were settled.

It was a terrible blow to his young wife with two children to be so suddenly reduced from affluence to poverty... . But, there was a friend at hand—London. He had secured a situation as teamster with a wholesale house that had resumed business in the city; and every Saturday evening found him at the door of the house in which Mrs. Bale lived with packages of tea, coffee, sugar, butter, etc., such as she had been accustomed to and could no longer afford to buy; bought with his own money, from the same exclusive establishment where she formerly dealt. Occasionally when passing that way with his truck he would leave a ham at the door. This continued until the death of the lady. Tom Bale never returned. It was said he fell a victim to malaria and died in a far away land.

It is but a few years since London went to his reward. He became a deacon in his church before he died, and on many a Thursday night meeting he would stand and sing:—
"What troubles have we seen
What conflicts have we passed!
But out of all the Lord
Has brought us by his love.
And still he doth his grace
Afford, and hides our lives above."[4]
while tears of gratitude rolled down his cheeks. He had lived to dwell "under his own vine and fig tree, with none to molest or make him afraid."[5]

4   This is a version of lyrics to the hymn "Are We Yet Alive."
5   This is a phrase quoted in the Hebrew scripture in various places, but here it may be from Micah 4:4.

CHAPTER X

Silla—The Maid

"As we forgive those who trespass against us."[1]

I t is more pleasant to me than otherwise that I have no other similar instance of cruelty to relate, coming under my own observation like that of Tom Bale's. Although the following may not be called cruel, still it is not devoid of severity and harshness.

Among our neighbors there was a family whose servants had rather a hard time of it. This family was very religious but not liberal minded. All their servants had to attend the family church.

One of the ladies had a maid whose lot was hard indeed.[2] She was only allowed to wear such dresses as her mistress prescribed, and these were always made of the coarsest material after an original design. She was never permitted to wear a bonnet, but must have her head tied with a bandanna. No idea of economy prompted the mistress. There were those mean enough to say that it was done because Silla was very pretty and the lady was so plain.

Now the maid was fond of dress. She also had strong religious sentiments. She was also an expert needle-woman, and her brother who "hired

---

1   The Lord's Prayer, Matthew 6:9–13.
2   Silla was enslaved by "Mrs. Tom Bale," who was likely of the Boyle family.

his time" and "worked out," furnished her with material which she fashioned to suit herself—working at night and at odd times. Sometimes on Sundays she managed to attend the church of her choice, arrayed in such garments as she desired, being careful however, to leave the house after the family had gone, and to return before their arrival. But she came to grief at last.

It was during a season of great excitement in religious circles in the city. The Baptists were making heavy inroads on the Methodist Camp, and the latter found it necessary to bring out their heavy artillery. Many eminent Divines noted for their piety, learning and eloquence had been invited by the Methodist clergy to assist in calming the fears of their flocks. Silla was a strong Methodist, therefore when it was announced that on a certain Sunday a Reverend Gentlemen of matchless eloquence would preach, she determined to hear him. It was said that this particular sermon had the effect of sending the wavering ones back to their ranks; for, after an impassioned appeal to his hearers to stand firm, he closed his eloquent discourse as follows:—

> "Let others glory in the water
> I glory in the blood."[3]

I need not tell you that on that Sunday Silla appeared in a beautiful dress made in the latest style, a rich mantilla, and a bonnet that was not inexpensive. Altogether she presented a very enviable appearance.[4]

When she was ready to start out, Aunt Cinda, the old nurse, said to her, "Now gal, yo luk berry nice indeed, but doan le dem tings tun yo hed so de buckra git home fo yo."[5]

"O no ma'am, Aunt Cinda, I'll be in time."

But alas! What with a word of greeting here, and a word of congratulation there, after service, the time slipped by. As Silla sped homeward she

---

3   This appears to be a paraphrase of a notion about ultimately revering and placing faith only in Jesus's "blood sacrifice."
4   A mantilla would be a scarf, possibly lace, draped around the neck, shoulders, and hair.
5   Aunt Cinda: An elderly enslaved woman.

became aware of the fact that she was late. She quickened her pace, but "Time lost can never be regained."[6] Miss Octavia had reached home before she got there.[7]

On reaching the house the lady had immediately called for her maid, and was quite surprised to find that she had not yet returned from church. Therefore, she took her seat on the piazza which commanded a full view of the servants' entrance, determined to ascertain from Silla as soon as she came in, the meaning of her tardiness. The lady was not in a pleasant frame of mind either, as she was quite thirsty and wanted a drink of water.

As Silla timidly opened the gate and put her head in she would have withdrawn it, but … "Walk in here, madam!" came from her mistress in tones that were not to be misunderstood, "Where have you been?"

"To church, ma'am."

"What church, pray?"

"Methodist, ma'am."

"And who gave you those horrid things you have on?"

"Bobber Jim, ma'am."[8]

"He did, eh! Come right in here."

Silla's heart sank within her as she meekly obeyed. Miss Octavia followed her servant into the house. "Get me some old newspapers," she said. "Place them in that grate. Take off that hat and lay it on the paper. Now get a match and set the fire." And the poor girl stood there and saw her beautiful bonnet go up in smoke.

"Now madam, go a take off those things and never let me see you with them on again!"

Silla served Miss Octavia for a long time after the war. The lady is dead now, but the maid is still living in Charleston, South Carolina.

---

6   A common proverb of unknown origins.

7   "Mrs. Tom Bale": Tormenter of Silla.

8   Silla's brother or perhaps a free Black laborer in Charleston who had money to give her gifts. It is also remotely possible that the dialect here was meant to invoke pronunciation of "father" Jim and to suggest that he was a preacher of some sort.

CHAPTER XI

The Appraisement

"He will give His angels charge concerning thee."[1]

While we were at Mrs. Bale's and before I went "into camp," I had the following sad experience:—Up to this event it had never dawned upon me that my condition was not as good as that of any boy in the country.[2] With kind parents, two sweet little sisters, an affectionate brother, gentle companions to play with, and every boyish wish gratified, the improbability of my succession to the presidential chair never occurred to me. But now I was made to feel that life was not all "one pleasant dream."

One day my mother received a message calling her down to the Dane's. When she returned she seemed very sad, and upon my father's arrival home I saw them in earnest conversation. Before I went to bed that night my mother told me that I would have to go with her to the Dane's on the next day. "The Old Jay wants to see you," she said.[3]

---

1   Psalms 91:11–12.

2   The time shifts in this memoir move swiftly, and here we see him returning again to a time before he was sent to serve the Army officers in the Secessionville encampment.

3   This would be the nickname for "Mrs. Dane" or Mrs. Dias.

I was greatly pleased at this for it was a long time since I had been there. When we arrived the next day I found all the servants arrayed as if for some holiday occasion and I also found that they were to be "praised."[4] However, I couldn't understand why persons dressed up as they were, and who had been brought together for commendation, should look so sad. I did not know what I had done deserving of special mention, but I did remember that sometime before my horse ran away with my through the crowded streets, and that I had managed to keep my seat. I finally brought the animal to a stand without any damage. Therefore, I thought I would receive a gold medal, or perhaps "four pence" in money. But to be certain, I would ask Cora what it all meant.

I found her seated alone on a bench in the yard looking more beautiful than ever. "Cora," said I, "What is all of this about?" … Instead of answering my question she began to cry and she took hold of me and hugged and kissed me right there in the yard, before all those people!! My, didn't I blush!

The fact was, kind reader, as you have already surmised, the "Estate" was to be sold, and the people had been brought together for "appraisement."

Several gentlemen came out into the yard. The people stood up, and the gentlemen went among them asking questions. One of them placed his hand on my head… . "Well, my boy," said he, "What can you do?"

"I can ride, Sir," I answered, whereupon my mother gave me a gentle nudge which meant, "Hush." She then explained to him that my brother and I were not to be sold for she had earnestly requested Mr. Dane not to "sell" us. She knew that we should receive good treatment as long as we were in his hands, and that if we went with her, the Negro Traders would soon separate us. With many protestations Mr. Dane had promised her that he would not sell us even if he had to go barefoot. He kept his word, but my mother and two little sisters went and for four years, we neither saw nor heard of each other. When "the cruel war was over" we were brought together again, and you may know there was a happy meeting for—"He had given his angels charge concerning us."—We were all there to greet the gallant Major Anderson when he returned to raise the "Old Flag" over Fort Sumter.[5]

---

4   He is depicting the way a child might misunderstand the word "appraised."
5   "When the cruel war was over" was a common phrase of the period. "He had given his angels …" is a nod to Psalms 91:11, and Major Anderson was, as

>"'Twas the star spangled banner
> And long may it wave,
> O'er the land of the free
> And the home of the brave."[6]

The war was ended. The Union had come. Soon the schools were thrown open, and under the leadership of the enthusiastic Redpath, and that noble band of pioneer men and women from the North, the children flocked to them.[7] Surely there must be a future for a people so eager to learn as is the Negro, and though we are not yet out of the woods,

> "We are coming, Father Abraham
> Full many a million strong."[8]

mentioned earlier in the narrative, the Federal Officer who had been forced to surrender Fort Sumter, on April 13, 1861.

6   Williams here invokes his own version of the national anthem, "The Star-Spangled Banner."

7   James Redpath (1833–91) was a journalist and an antislavery activist, who, in February 1865, was appointed by Federal military authorities as the Superintendent of Schools for Charleston, South Carolina. Williams also makes a gesture to the men and women from the North who came South to work as teachers for emancipated slave children.

8   This is the second time Williams has quoted this popular song, "We are Coming Father Abraham," but in this instance he is referring to the millions of freed men and women hoping to claim their future in the United States as educated citizens.

CHAPTER XII

The Big Fire

"Hear the loud alarum bell."[1]

On the night of December 11th, 1861, our dear old home on Guignard street was destroyed by fire. This was the greatest conflagration that has happened in Charleston during my lifetime.[2]

It broke out at, or near the corner of East Bay and Hasel Streets, and swept in a direction across the city to the very edge of Ashley River, at the other side of town; licking up nearly everything in its patch. When the alarm was given Ward 3, we hurried out from Mrs. Bate's where we were living at that time.[3] Not very far away from the old place, looking in that direction, we saw the flames leaping up, and hastened on. The sparks seemed to rain down from the heavens as we ran. When we reached there,

---

1   This is evidently a quotation from Edgar Allen Poe's poem of 1849, "The Bells."

2   This account of Charleston's devastating fire of 1861, often known as "The Great Fire," is a rare perspective of the event from an enslaved person. Note that in this chapter Williams has again shifted time sequences and is moving from his discussion about the end of the war back to the early years of the war, namely 1861.

3   "Mrs. Bate's" might have been a boarding house.

we found the engines pouring streams of water on the house, while there was a long line of men reaching from the well in the yard, up the back stairs to the roof of the house, passing buckets of water from one to another.

The devoted ladies stood by encouraging them. "Water! More water!" they cried. But it was all unavailing. The fire soon caught the piazzas, then burst in the windows and doors seeming to say, "Who would stay the 'Fire King?'"[4] Soon the old home together with nearly all of the neighboring houses was a mass of ruin. On swept the flames reaching Broad Street. They raged about the Cathedral.[5] It was thought that owing to the material of which that beautiful structure was built, it would have escaped, but no—under the fierce onslaught of the devouring element, the costly and magnificent edifice melted away; and onward the fire sped, not stopping until it reached the waters of the Ashley River.

I do not know the casualties that attended this distressing event, but the property loss was very great.

4   The specific reference here is unknown, but Williams is emphasizing the way in which the fire appeared to be an animated being.

5   Williams is certainly thinking of The Roman Catholic Cathedral of St. John and St. Finbar, located on Broad Street in Charleston, which was destroyed by the 1861 fire.

CHAPTER XIII

Mr. Ward's Return to Pine Top

"Let us have peace."[1]

It was late in the Fall of 1865 that Mr. Ward was on his way to join his family. As soon as possible after the surrender at Richmond, he had made a hasty visit to Charleston to assure himself of their safety, but had returned to Richmond after a few days stay with them to engage in some clerical work he had previously secured in that city; the compensation for which he found himself sorely in need of at that time. He was now on his way to join them permanently. He had an irresistible impulse however to visit the old plantation. As the train sped on, the desire grew upon him, therefore, when they pulled up at the little station, White House, he got off, determined to walk out to the place.[2] It is worthy of note that this man did not for a moment doubt that he would be kindly received by his former slaves, if any remained there.

---

1   General Ulysses S. Grant's campaign slogan of 1868 was "let us have peace."
2   This station was likely an informal stop (since it isn't listed in the regional railroad guides of that era). It would most probably have been on the South Carolina Canal and Railroad Line coming out of Charleston and would have been a short carriage ride to "Pine Top" plantation labor camp or what was actually known as the Pine Hill property.

Fortunately he met an old friend at the station who gladly provided him with a horse on which he rode out to the plantation, beset by emotions better imagined than described. As he turned from the road into the long avenue a mass of ruins met his eyes. The noble old house had been destroyed by fire! With a sad heart he rode on.

Uncle Joe was at work burning stubble in a nearby field. As he raised his eyes they rested on the lone horseman. "Wonder who da him," he said as he started to meet the stranger, "Um, ee luk like Mass Willum, Lord bless me!"

As the two men drew near each other Mr. Ward leaped from his horse and extending his hand he cried, "Joe!"

They fell on each others necks and wept like children. Oh why did the designing stranger and the native demagogue enter to thwart this auspicious opening of a new era between these men?[3]

After a while they started toward Uncle Joe's cabin. Mr Ward refused to remount though urged to do so by the old man. As they walked along Mr. Ward inquired about those he had left on the place. Some had gone away. They had sought the city. It were well for many of these if they had remained on the plantation, for the town held many snares and temptations to which they were unaccustomed, and to which they fell a prey. Old Uncle Josh and his wife had gone to Mrs. Ward in Charleston. Uncle Josh was not inclined to leave the plantation, but his wife was anxious to go and see how Mrs. Ward was faring, and if she could be of any help to her. Thus they went.

Mrs. Ward was more than glad to see her old friends. "I thank you very much for coming to me at this time," she said to Aunt —, but I am not able to offer you any wages, for I am without means now."

"I a'int cum fer yo money, Chile," the old woman answered, "Ef yo doan need my sarbis I ken go back."

"Oh you dear old creature, you know how much I need you. I only meant that I cannot pay you anything just now."

---

3   It is not entirely clear, but it appears that Williams is trying to speculate about why Reconstruction went so poorly in South Carolina when a new era between enslavers and the formerly enslaved could have been marked with love. He blames the failure of reconciliation on the interlopers (presumably from the North) and local agitators (presumably native to the South).

And so the old woman took charge, greatly to the relief of Mrs. Ward, also to that of Uncle August who had been constantly with his mistress, and was acting in the capacity of general house servant. The advent of Aunt Peggy allowed him a chance to go out doing odd jobs, thereby earning a few dollars. He steadily refused to accept any work that would take him away permanently from Mrs. Ward. The lady could offer comfortable quarters to Uncle Josh and his wife. The old man soon obtained work in the city and the three servants lived on the premises until they died. It is doubtful if Mrs. Ward ever had any more faithful and truer servants than they were.

Mr. Ward was glad to find that there were still many of his people on the plantation, all of whom seemed glad to see him. Old Aunt Binah, Uncle Joe's wife was dead, and his two boys, now strapping young fellows had gone to the city to work. "Long shore" the old man informed him, also that they had turned out well and came up to see him often.[4]

As they neared the cabin they passed a pen in which were six fine shoats "Dem b'long to Mingo, sah," said Uncle Joe.[5]

A shade passed over Mr. Ward's face. "Mingo?" he asked.

"Yessah. Mingo mar'ed Dolly, yo kno sah, an ee com ter lib yer wid er. And den wen they gon ter town an my old ooman dead, Dolly un him com lib wid me sah, caise I so lonsum. Mingo is er good christon man sah, an dey berry kine ter me."

The shade on Mr. Ward's face deepened. "Joe," said he, "I treated Mingo harshly once."

"I kno dat, but ee don forgit all bou it, sah."

Mr. Ward sighed as though he wished he could forget also. "Is Lucy still here?" he asked.

"Yee, sah. She es prime es eber."

"Let us go over and see her."

"Praise de Lawd!" cried the old woman as they entered her cabin. Mr. Ward could not speak, but extended his hand.

"Mas Willum, I'se berry glad ter see yer. Si' down. How yer bin all dis time?"

---

4   This suggests that Joe's sons were then employed at the Charleston docks unloading or loading cargo onto boats.

5   "Shoats" are young pigs.

"Well, Ma'am Lucy, I have had some hard raps, but I am thankful to be alive, and to see you all again. A great change has come about."

"Yees sah, God mov een er misterous way."

After a short stay at Aunt Lucy's they visited the other cabins before returning to Uncle Joe's abode. "Sorry de ole ooman ain't yere, sah," said the old man with moistened eyes, as they went in. Dolly, busy with the housework, had noticed Uncle Joe and a white man going to the barn with a horse. They had left the horse there and were next seen coming toward the cabin. With native shyness she drew herself from view, and when she ventured to peep out again, the man had passed her house going in the direction of Aunt Lucy's. "Vonder who dat," she had said, and went on with her work.

Meanwhile Mr. Ward and Uncle Joe had completed their visits and returned. She did not see them until they entered the rear door of the cabin. She was just about to put a large dish into the cupboard when she glanced up... . Down went the dish to the floor in a hundred pieces!!! "Don't be frightened, Dolly," said Mr. Ward, smiling and extending his hand. "You got your Mingo after all."

Dolly was speechless for a moment. Then she said, "Ee this you Moas Willum!"

"Yes indeed," replied the gentleman, "and I am truly glad to see you. How are you and your husband?"

"Ve quite well, tankee sah. How yo do?"

"Oh, I feel better now, than I have for many a day," he replied.

The men sat down before the blazing fire and entered into a long and earnest conversation concerning the past, the present and the future. Just before they entered the door, Mr. Ward had noticed a fine possum hanging outside, all cleaned and ready for the oven. He was at the point of expressing his delight at the sight when he was arrested by the pathetic remarks of Uncle Joe. During a lull in the conversation he turned to Dolly and said, "I see you have a fine possum."

"Yees sah," she answered, "Mingo ketch him las night, and gwine ter hab im for supper. Glad yo cum jest cen time."

"I am glad too, said Mr. Ward laughingly.

Mingo worked at the ferry half a mile away. He was later than usual coming home that evening, and had reached the house without being apprised of Mr. Ward's arrival. When he came in and saw the gentleman, he stood motionless with astonishment. Mr. Ward got up. Advancing toward the bewildered man with outstretched hand he said, " Mingo, I treated you harshly once. I am ashamed of it, and I wish to ask your pardon."

Mingo grasped his hand. "Doan say nothin bout dat, sah. Ise glad ter see yo—berry glad ter see yo sah. Si down." And the two men had a long talk.

CHAPTER XIV

Roast Possum

"Tun dat possum roun and roun
Tun dat possum roun."[1]

Dolly knew the high estimate Mr. Ward had of old Aunt Lucy's ability as a cook, therefore she requested her to come over that evening. This the old lady readily consented to do, and as she proceeded with her pleasant task, she indulged in many reminiscences of former occasions on which she had officiated to the gastronomic delight of Mr. Ward; and even of old Mr. Bale, Mrs. Ward's father. When everything was ready Dolly brought out a snowy cloth, spread it on the pine table, laid a plate, knife and fork thereon, then she ran down to the spring for some fresh water. Returning, she placed a glass of this beside the plate. Meanwhile Aunt Lucy was taking up the supper. On a large dish she gently placed the festive possum done to a turn. Then she carefully arranged some baked sweet potatoes around it. Over all she poured some gravy that had been simmering in a saucepan by the fire. She placed this dish in front of the plate on the table, and flanked it on one side by a dish of rice as white as milk, and on the other by some delicious cornbread. She surveyed the table a moment then announced, "Supper ready."

1 This appears to be a version of "Carve dat Possum," a popular minstrel song written in 1875 by Sam Lucas.

"Draw up, sah," said Mingo acting as master of ceremonies.

"Surely you are all going to join me!" said Mr. Ward rising.

"No sah," answered Uncle Joe, "It do ve mo good ter see yo eat dan ter eat veself, sah."

Argument was of no avail, therefore Mr. Ward sat down and in a remarkably short space of time that dish of possum and potatoes had very perceptively diminished. After Mr. Ward was through, the table was rearranged and the others sat down.[2]

The gentleman looked thoughtfully into the fire, and when all had finished he stood up. "Joe, Lucy, Mingo, Dolly," said he, calling each by name, "I can never hope to enjoy another meal such as I have had, as long as I live. His earnestness impressed them all. They made no reply.

Immediately after supper Mingo had excused himself, and was absent for more than an hour. All of those whom Mr. Ward had not seen during the day came in after supper to shake hands with him. Mingo was seen to whisper to two or three of the younger men, and together they went out; seemingly on some mysterious errand.

Some of the older people tarried a while to talk. "Chillun," said Aunt Lucy, "Look at de venders ob de Master." Then she raised her voice an sang, "And are we yet alive?"

Uncle Joe requested the old woman to pray. They all knelt down while she uttered a prayer of wonderful strength; full of faith and hope. Mr. Ward was asked by the old man to read the 14th chapter of St. John.[3] Uncle Joe, though still vigorous, was quite an old man; therefore, at the conclusion of the reading he sang:—

> "On Jordan's stormy banks I stand
> And cast a wistful eye."[4]

---

2   The Black and white people involved here are carefully following the protocol of racial hierarchy, and even though the War is recently over and the Emancipation of all the formerly enslaved people should have taken effect they make sure the former master eats first before they then sit down and eat their own meals, even though they are the "hosts" of this event.

3   Jesus comforts his disciples in John 14.

4   Williams here references the hymn "On Jordan's Stormy Banks," written by Samuel Stennett and originally titled "The Promised Land."

They all felt that he was looking, "For a house not made with hands, but eternal in the heavens." And so he was, for a few months later he passed on to his reward.

They had all joined in the singing and accustomed as was Mr. Ward to hearing them, it seemed as though he was never so impressed as now. Again and again he requested them to sing, and they responded with such old hymns as:—

> "Roll Jordan, roll
> My bruder, yo aught to bin dere
> To yer wen Jordan roll."[5]

When they rose to leave they sang heartily:—

> "No fearin, no doubtin
> While God's on our side.
> We'll all die er shoutin'
> De Lawd will provide."[6]

Kind reader have you ever heard of those people sing? If a band of these old veterans could be brought together and travel through the country singing their old time songs, I believe it would do more towards settling the so called Negro problem, and allaying the growing unrest caused thereby, than any other single force. The particular ones of whom I write are all, with a single exception, dead; but there are still many of the "Old Timers" living.

Mr. Ward had not expected to stay long, but the hours sped swiftly, and he was forced to spend the night under the roof of old Uncle Joe.

5   Williams here references the hymn "Roll, Jordan, Roll," originally written by Charles Wesley and adapted and sung by African American slaves. See Kelsey Anderson, "The History and Reception of 'Roll Jordan, Roll,'" "Music 345: Race, Identity, and Representation in American Music," Student Blogs and Library Exhibit, March 20, 2018: https://pages.stolaf.edu/americanmusic/2018/03/20/the-history-and-reception-of-roll-jordan-roll/.
6   These lyrics are from "The Lord Will Provide," a commonly known evangelical hymn of the nineteenth century.

Mr. Mingo went to work early the next morning before Mr. Ward was up.

The borrowed horse had been returned by one of the men going to the station, as the gentleman found his stay would be prolonged. Uncle Joe would drive him over to take the train.

After breakfast Uncle Joe went to the barn to "hitch up." When he drove up to the cabin door there was a large homespun sack which seemed to contain something bulky, lying across the rear part of the buggy. "Got quite a load behind you, Joe," remarked Mr. Ward as he stepped in.

"One ob Mingo shoats, sah. Ee kill im las night. Say ee sorry ee didn't hab time to cut up de meat. Yo kin hab dat don wen yo git home. Hang im up in er cool place, sah."

The gentleman made no reply, but there was a strange, far away look in his eyes. As they drove, the old man imparted such bits of information as he thought might be of interest. Finally both became silent. "Joe," at length said Mr. Ward, "You are thoughtful as usual."

"Fine nuff ter tink bout, sah. Member once wen I didn't tink, an ee put de wuk on de plantation bac two days." He laughed loudly as though amused by some recollection. Mr. Ward smilingly asked when this happening had occurred. Then the old man related the circumstances which were as follows:—

Mr. Ward had directed him to have a piece of work done. He had delayed in doing it because there was something about it to which he wished to call his master's attention. However, before he could do so Mr. Ward called him and demanded to know what was the cause of the delay. "I thought sah," began Uncle Joe. "I don't want you to think. Do as I tell you," Mr. Ward had said sternly.

Later the old man's reasons were discovered to be well founded, but his master made no acknowledgment of it. One morning some time after Mr. Ward had said, "Joe, tomorrow morning early, take two double teams and four men, and go over to Mr. Bennett Ward's (a brother of his).[7] There are some things there; furniture, etc., that I wish to have brought here. Make a very early start. I will ride over after you. Wait there until I come."

---

7   Mr. Bennett Ward: "Mr. Ward's" or Mr. Waring's brother.

Now it so happened that on this very day, after Mr. Ward had given his instructions, he received a letter calling him to the city on urgent business. He went down that evening. Naturally he said nothing to Uncle Joe, nor did he change his orders. The old man knew he was gone, also that it was impossible for him to return in time to ride over to his brother's, as it was eight miles across the country. But he was not to think!

By daylight next morning, he with teams and men, was on the road to "Mas' Bennett." On his arrival he told the gentleman the orders he had received from his master. "All right," said he, "Wait." And they waited.

At dinner time Mr. Ward expressed surprise that his brother had not come. At night he felt worried about it. "If he is not here in the morning I shall ride over and see what the matter is," he said.

The next day, when breakfast had been completed, he mounted his horse and rode away, telling Joe to remain there as his brother might come at any moment. He had expected to meet Mr. William on the way, but after riding several miles without doing so, he became quite alarmed and went on to Pine Top. His brother he found, had been called to the city unexpectedly, and had not returned as yet. Mrs. Ward knew that her husband intended to send Joe, but thought he had altered the arrangement when he found that he would be absent. She was just on the verge of sending for Joe to come back.

It was near three o'clock when Mr. Ward got home. His brother was in the act of leaving. "I did tell Joe to go over to your place yesterday, and to wait until I came. I forgot all about it until a few moments ago. When you get home, please see that the wagons are loaded tonight, and let them start back by daylight," said Mr. William Ward.[8]

Not until nine o'clock in the morning of the third day of their absence did they return to Pine Top. Work had been terribly put back on the place. But, Uncle Joe had done as he was told, without thinking.

Mr. Ward remembered facts distinctly. He now learned for the first time the true inwardness of them. "Joe," said he with a smile, "That was not the only mistake I ever made."

They bade each other good-bye at the station. "Remain on the plantation, Joe, and tell all the others to do so until we can see what is to be done," said Mr. Ward as he boarded the train. They never met again!

8   Evidently a brother of "Mr. Ward." He was possibly a relative of Waring.

Mr. Ward entered the ministry and labored for some years on the coast among his own people, in the vicinity where he once had his military headquarters. Was the inspiration furnished by that memorable visit to the old plantation? Who can tell?

CHAPTER XV

After De Union

"Universal Suffrage say to all, Be ye tranquil."[1]

Reconstruction times were now at hand. The ruinous conditions that followed that period have been oft and repeatedly charged to the Negroes of South Carolina. Is this just? Is it true? I say, No! I was but a boy then. I remember going with my father who was one of a delegation of men selected for the purpose of calling on some gentlemen of Charleston. These gentlemen, although they had been slaveholders, were always kindly disposed toward the Negro. I understand that the purpose of the visits was to secure the good offices of these gentlemen in framing new laws for the government of the state.

The first one they called on came out and stood uncovered on the doorsteps, while the spokesman of the Negroes explained the object of the visit. The venerable gentleman thanked the delegates for this expression of their confidence, and promised to do all in his power to bring about peace and tranquility to the state and people.

They made other visits with like results. "Bless be the man who ne'er consents by ill advice to walk," is as applicable to a state of community

---

1   This was a common Reconstruction-era rallying cry known throughout the South, reminding people that with the vote would come a peaceful future.

as to an individual.[2] Ill advice seemed to have ruled the first attempt at legislation in South Carolina after the war; for the outcome of it was the enactment of the Negroes in the state worse if possible, than it was under slavery. These laws were very appropriately called, "The Black Code."[3] It is strange that we do not hear much of that code now. Possibly somebody is ashamed of it.

That was the entering wedge. It opened the door to the designing stranger, and made subsequent conditions possible. It was not the work of the Negroes, but it opened the way for, and brought about, what is called the "Carpet Bag"[4] era, of which nothing good can be said. It was "Bad," very "Bad."

But the state was finally wrested from the hands of the despoiler. The gallant Hampton came to the rescue.[5] About this time men who had found things under the corrupt Carpet Bag System, "as sweet as a daisy in a cow's mouth," awoke to the discovery that the "Civilization of the Cavalier and the Roundhead was imperiled."[6] This discovery it was said, was hastened by the

2   This was a Psalm that was also used in various hymns, so Williams could be quoting directly from the Bible or from one of the many hymns that evidently occupied his imagination.

3   When referring to the "Black Code," Williams means the laws enacted by the Southern states after the Civil War. These codes were laws which were put into place to limit African Americans' freedom. For example, South Carolina laws required proof of employment by January in the form of a contract. If an African American left before the contract was up, their pay would be docked, and they could be subject to arrest. See "The Southern 'Black Codes' of 1865–66": www. crf-usa.org/brown-v-board-50th-anniversary/southern-black-codes.html.

4   "The Carpet Bag era" is a reference to "Carpetbaggers," a term used for Northerners who came to the South during Reconstruction in order to attempt to gain political power. As travelers from afar, they would carry luggage, often carpet bags.

5   "The gallant Hampton" refers to Wade Hampton, a former Confederate general. He strongly opposed Reconstruction and served as Governor of South Carolina during 1877–79.

6   Williams is paraphrasing a quotation made by Governor Daniel Henry Chamberlin of South Carolina, a Massachusetts Republican who had led a Black Regiment in the Civil War. Chamberlin sought to fight corruption and patronage in South Carolina and promote Civil Rights but created enemies among Black Republicans and white Democrats alike. The quotation here was evidently made

thought that their own heads were no less so. In fact, in Charleston today, a highly respected gentleman and citizen is living, who in a public speech said in effect, "Let us not blame the Negroes; they have been but dupes. Let us rather ornament the lamp posts of the city with the suspended bodies of the rascals who have used them for their own selfish purposes."[7]

At that time I was a young man in the employment of one of the oldest business firms in Charleston. One day one of my employers called me into his private office. (This gentleman was one of the most conscientious men I have ever known. He had been very kind to me, as indeed were all the members of the firm. In all my varied experiences I have never with kinder treatment than I received at their hands). After telling me of the deplorable condition in which the state then was, he asked me to support General Wade Hampton for governor, in the coming election. I told him that while I realized the truth of what he had said, I could not vote for Hampton! Also, that in consequence of the chaotic conditions in the state I had determined not to vote at all.[8] He then asked me if I would go to hear General Hampton, (the general was to speak especially to the Negroes of Charleston). This I readily consented to do.

I do not remember the date of this meeting. It was however, a short time before the election which took place on the seventh day of November, 1876. At the appointed time the Academy of Music was crowded with the Negroes of the city.[9] I could only get standing room. We, the Negroes, could sit in any part of the place we desired then.

when he refused to appoint two Southern Democrats (and former Confederates) to a circuit court.

7   Historian Paul Anderson of Clemson University has speculated that this reference might be from a speech by Charleston Mayor Ashmead Courtenay (1831–1908) or possibly wealthy Charleston businessman and Philanthropist Andrew Murray (1844–1928). Paul Anderson, "Courtenay citation?" email (2020).

8   Williams registered to vote in 1877, which suggests he did not vote for Wade Hampton or anyone else in 1876. Whether he actually went on to vote in 1877 or beyond is unknown but he and his father are clearly listed in the Charleston Election Ledger of 1877 currently held by the Charleston County Public Library.

9   The Academy of Music was certainly the Owens Academy of Music in Charleston, South Carolina. Comedian John Owens bought the theater that was originally there in 1875 and renamed it the "Owens Academy of Music."

General Wade Hampton rose to speak—a splendid man, a perfect specimen of manhood and vigor. The hardships of the war through which he had passed seemed to have had but little effect upon him. He was a fluent speaker. In a forceful manner he told of the sad condition in which the affairs of the state then stood. Our only desire he said, was to save our dear old state from utter ruin. Then, raising his right hand to heaven he said these very words as near as I can recollect, "If I am elected governor, I swear to God that not one right or privilege that you now enjoy shall be taken from you!"

I believe, in fact I know he was sincere, and while I did not vote for him I honored his sincerity. But he had made pledges for his people which they failed to keep. The immediate result of his election was the passing of restrictive measures aimed exclusively at the Negro. The brave old general lived to see the day when he, like his pledges, was laid aside—a soldier and a gentleman. It was well for him that he was bred in the school of the solider; well for him that he was truly brave, else he could not have stood up against it.

"He was a man take him in all for all"

and I fear, we in South Carolina,

"May not look upon his like again."[10]

But the end is not yet, for we hear of other oppressive measures, such as disfranchisement and the like. While this is true it is equally true that the Negro has many friends among the southern white people. Such offensive measures as the "Jim Crow Car," are not the works of the better element of the southern people.[11] Many Negroes owe their success in business enterprises and other efforts they have put forward for their advancement, directly to the aid and encouragement they have received from those who formerly held them in bondage.

10   Shakespeare's *Hamlet* (Act 1, scene 2).
11   This would have been a racially segregated seating area on some form of public transportation, likely a coach, carriage, or train car.

If there is a Negro problem before the American people, it is one of the greatest propositions that has ever confronted them. If either of the measures yet proposed could be carried out it would not settle the Negro question, for I hear of no plan yet to remove the Negro from the face of the earth. Though, perhaps even this would find many advocates. If there is a Negro problem, a great principle is involved in its settlement. There is no question of the power of the white people of America to dispose of it in any way they may choose, but, to "settle it," requires the exercise of justice and equity.

To many this problem seems more imaginary than real, and the measures thus far proposed for its settlement seem impractical to say the least of them. One-sided settlements are hardly ever satisfactory or conclusive.

If this is a real vital question it effects the Negro as well as the white man, and the simple principles of humanity and "fair play" would seem to call for the consideration and the interest of both.

Why not call the brains of the Negro into the council for its consideration? There is plenty of it among the men of large caliber, many whose names are frequently before the public, and others whose names are seldom heard. I believe they would convince the country, and the world that this "Great Lion" is no more formidable than those which "Pilgram" saw.[12]

When a boy I knew a man whom I greatly disliked. I did not know anything wrong about him, but there was something about his looks that repulsed me. I never cared to meet him. Some time afterwards I learned something of his history. He had been shipwrecked once. Together with some others he got into a small boat. As they pulled off from the sinking vessel a strong swimmer reached the boat and tried to climb in. This man violently struck the hands of the swimmer away, and the poor fellow

12   This misspelling and quotation appears to be a call out to John Bunyan's allegorical Christian work of 1687, *Pilgrim's Progress*. In one scene of that book, the hero, Christian, is fearful of walking between lions in a narrow pathway. He is told they are chained and won't quite be able to reach him, but he must, as an act of faith, walk between them. He gathers up his courage and makes his way through them. If this is the reference, Williams is suggesting that the problems of reconciling race antagonism and injustice are not as terrible as they may appear.

sank beneath the waves. He justified himself on the ground that there was already a sufficient number in the boat, and if the swimmer had not been prevented from entering the boat, the lives of these would have been endangered. Perhaps he was right, but I was more afraid of him than ever, for I could not think of him as other than a murderer.

Those who would drive the Negro away from this country for which he has fought and bled, I regard as worse than this man; for, we are all ready in the boat, and they seek to cast us into the sea.

CHAPTER XVI

In the Land of the Puritans

"'Tis a very good land I tell you,
'Tis a very fine land indeed."[1]

For years I had desired to visit "away down east."[2] I wanted to see more of those people from whom sprung the liberty-loving men and women, who did so much for the amelioration of the condition of the race. I had all ready witnessed the practical working of their christian charity, and the zeal through the labor of that gallant band, who immediately after the war came down to the south with the bible in one hand, and the primer in the other; for the purpose of enlightening and elevating a benighted people.

---

1   This editor has not been able to ascertain the origin of these lines. Perhaps a popular song of the era.
2   This might be a reference to the region of Maine and Vermont. A popular film directed by D. W. Griffith in 1920 titled *Way Down East* and starring Lillian Griffith (and filmed partly in Vermont) might also be part of what Williams is referencing here. The film itself was based on a melodrama of 1898 so while the specific reference is unclear, it is fair to assume it was a popular phrase of the period when Williams was drafting his memoir.

They have nearly all passed away, for it is more than forty years since, but there remains as monuments to their philanthropy, the schools and colleges they established throughout the southland.

With the view therefore, of becoming better acquainted with these people, I availed myself of the first opportunity that presented itself. Before this I had visited some of their large cities, but the population of cities do not afford the opportunity of gaining such clear insight of a people as the country does. For, in the cities they are on "dress parade," but in the country they are "at home" so to speak, therefore, I wished to visit the rural or semi-rural parts of the country.

It is a "far cry" from the land of cotton and of rice to the land of pie and of beans. Yet, within four days after leaving my home in South Carolina, I found myself among the hills and mountains of one of the eastern states, and I seemed to have landed in the very heart of the "pie belt," as the following story will show.

Soon after my arrival I entered the services of a gentleman, and was assigned to duty at some distance from his residence. It was too far away for me to return to the house for dinner, so I provided with an ample "dinner pail" which the cook arranged for me each morning before I left the house. The first day when I opened my pail at noon, I found some delicious bread and butter, a generous slice of cake, a piece of pie, and a bottle of rich milk. You may be sure I enjoyed this very much indeed. On the second day there were cake, bread, and pie, and on the third day pie, bread, and cake.

Now, I had thought I was somewhat partial to pie, having been accustomed to an occasional bite of that delicacy at home, but this was "too much." There were more than a dozen men engaged at the place, and I discovered that each one of them was as abundantly supplied with pie as myself. At this time there was a dear relative of mine engaged with the same family.[3] She saw how things were going with me, and one night when I returned from work, she surprised me with a dish of rice and tomatoes cooked in southern style. It was a revelation to the cook to see rice served in this manner, but it must have been a far greater revelation to her to see

---

3   Who this relative might have been is a bit of a mystery, but possibly it is the reason he left New York for work in Vermont.

how I devoured it. Soon my relative returned to her home in the south, and once more I found myself eating pie every day like a native.

The country was beautiful. It was in the famed Connecticut valley.[4] The coloring of the landscape was all that could be desired, but there was a lamentable lack of color in the population. This, you must know, was utterly unbearable to any man from South Carolina, be he white or black, unless it be our senior senator[5]. Therefore, I went to my employer and told him if the situation in this respect could not be changed, I could not remain in that part of the United States. "You see sir," said I, "I have a wife and ten children, and —."[6]

The gentleman leaped making a complete revolution in the air. "Ten children!" he exclaimed, "Where? What in the world!"

Here he seemed to recover his equilibrium. He had four or five children himself. I then explained to him that it was not my purpose to bring all of our children to Spring Lake, that there were ten children in our family, but five of them were at home, while the other five were doing well for themselves in another part of the States; that it was my intention to have my wife bring the five that were at home as far as New York, leave four of them there, and she and the youngest join me at Spring Lake for the present.[7] This arrangement suited him, and he promptly handed me a check covering the amount of their passage.

Before leaving home I had arranged with my wife that if I found my situation satisfactory, I would send for her, and that the arrangement for

4   Williams is referring to the Upper Connecticut River Valley located in Vermont (where it meanders down to the state of Connecticut).

5   It is possible that Williams's comment here refers to Benjamin Tillman, former senator from South Carolina and former slaveowner. Known for his racist views and defense of segregation, it is plausible that he would be happy to live only amongst white people.

6   This rather astonishing figure suggests that Williams had at that point a second wife, with perhaps some stepchildren, as well as older children from his first marriage. Since his first wife Mary Artsen Williams died in the mid-1880s, he likely married a second wife shortly thereafter. She may have had children from an earlier marriage.

7   "Spring Lake" is standing in for the city of Springfield, Vermont, where Williams and his family lived happily for several years.

the children indicated above, would be carried out. Consequently, it was with a light heart I wrote as follows:—

> "Dear H.
>
> I enclose check for —dollars. Come on north. Leave Tom, Dick, Harry and Betsy Ann with G— in New York, and you and Matilda Jane join me at Sorwind.[8]
>
> Your devoted husband."

But at the last moment our plans miscarried; and my wife found it necessary to bring all of the children with her.

The arrival of seven Afro-Americans created some excitement in the little town. I took my family to the Spring Lake Hotel and registered:— Mr. Sam Aleckson, wife and children, South Carolina. The next morning I explained the situation to my employer. He very readily, and with great kindness, placed at our disposal a neatly furnished cottage which he owned. How shall we ever thank the kind-hearted Miss M— who came personally to see that we were comfortably situated, and not in need of anything?

---

8   The "H" in this letter refers to his second wife. While my early research notes indicate her name was "Henrietta," I can no longer locate the exact documentation that would support that fact. Nonetheless, it is clear from the 1900 Federal census that Samuel Williams had been married twice and his second marriage had lasted for twelve years. Notably, the census in 1900 doesn't list his wife as living with him. She may have left him or perhaps she had died. The "G" name in this letter was possibly a relative of his or perhaps his second wife's relative. When he refers to "Sorwind," he is referencing either the county of Windsor in which the city of Springfield, Vermont, was located or the town of Windsor, Vermont, which was only sixteen miles from Springfield and where in later years he lived and wrote this memoir. These are not the real names of his children, or at least "Tom, Dick and Harry" appear to be joke names. Some of the children he is referring to may be children from his previous marriage, children with his second wife, or perhaps stepchildren. His first child, a boy, with Mary Artsen Williams, died as a baby in 1880, and he evidently had several other children, including Susan, with whom he seems to have lived the last forty years of his life. He also had a son, Samuel B. Williams Jr. and a daughter Carrie E. Williams, who all are listed along with their older sister Susan as living with Samuel Williams (and without their mother or stepmother) in the Windsor, Vermont, *City Directory* of 1905.

We began housekeeping under very favorable conditions. There was a large apple orchard around the house, and the children were as happy as larks. They had never before seen such an abundance of this delicious fruit. But our troubles were not yet over, as will hereafter appear.

We were quite comfortably situated. I had forgotten all about "pie," and we had resumed our old bill-of-fare: hominy, meat, bread, and tea or coffee for breakfast; meat, rice, and some vegetable for dinner, and bread, butter and tea for supper. One day a kind neighbor stepped in to see my wife. "I have just finished baking," she said, "I have made eight pies, a big pan of doughnuts, some cookies, and a cake. What kind of pie did you have for dinner?"

"Well er, oh, we didn't have any pie today."

"Good land, Mrs. Aleckson! No pie? What do you give those children to eat? Why, why!"

When I got home I found my wife looking worried. "What's troubling you?" I asked.

"Pie," she replied. Then she told me about the visit.

Next day I determined to consult a friend. After telling him my story he looked at me incredulously. "Well, now hain't you been having at least two kinds of pie every day right straight along?" he asked.

"Well no. You see er—er, um—" I began.

"Gosh, man!" he interrupted, "If you are going to stay here you will have to do it."

"Don't you think I might compromise on er, say, one every other day?" I asked helplessly.

"No siree! They might let you off on one each day, but I am not sure of that."

Again kind friends came to the rescue on the next night. When we were about to retire, there was a loud rap on the door. Upon opening it I saw a large delegation of neighbors, headed by our good friend Mrs. B—.[9] It was a surprise party, and they brought us material enough to make pies every day for two months!!!!

9   Mrs. B is the name of an unidentified Vermont neighbor.

CHAPTER XVII

The Town of Springlake

"Maud Miller on a Summer's Day."[1]

I found myself enjoying remarkable prosperity among a kind and hospitable people, who in industry, thrift and economy were unsurpassed.

Near our house there was a large meadow very suggestive of "Maude Miller" and the "Judge." The picture was heightened when I saw a buxom lass at work in the field. However, unlike Maud, she did not handle a rake. The raking is all done now by horse power. Instead she was provided with a fork which she wielded in "tumbling" with as much speed and dexterity as any of the men engaged in the work. She might, too, have proven an acquisition to the household of a judge, as I learned that she was a teacher of the higher branches in a high grade school, and only took this method during vacation to develop health and muscle. I felt sure if she had any rude boys in her class they would get the full benefit of it during the next school term.

The superiority of New England for house cleaning and housekeeping is well known. In house cleaning they excel. This they go about with absolute devotion. The spring house cleaning is scarcely over with when that of Fall begins. Indeed they seem to go about the house continually with

1   This is a reference to a poem by John Greenleaf Whittier called "Maude Muller."

hair broom and dustpan in hand. When any stray particle of dust is found, they swoop down upon it like a hawk does on a chicken, and bear it away in triumph to the furnace.

Ours is a great country; great in extent as well as in achievement. But, while many hundreds of miles may separate one community from another, still, through the means of the press and general literature we can readily obtain intelligence of our most distant neighbors. It is remarkable though, notwithstanding these sources of information, how our opinions, formed from what we have read of those at a distance from us, are apt to be altered, or completely changed by actual contact. It is also surprising to what extent people speaking the same language, living under practically the same institutions, and form of government, may differ in forms and customs. Here as elsewhere there are many peculiarities noticeable to the stranger.

Springlake is a historic old town. The public school system is perfect. There is a splendid library which adds greatly to the educational advantages of the place. It boasts of several churches. All the people in Springlake go to church, but I found in traveling through the country, the same falling off in church attendance as is noticeable in other parts of the United States—especially among the men.

When I was a school boy, there was a picture in one of my books that represented a man and woman walking through the forest. The woman held a book in her hand, while the man carried a gun; presumably a safeguard against attacks of wild beasts or savages. Indeed, if I remember rightly, there did appear the figure of an Indian peeping stealthily from behind a tree. The picture bore the title, "Going to Church in New England." The date given was sometime in the early settlement of the country. There seemed to be deep snow on the ground.

The devotion evinced by people attending church under such unfavorable conditions attracted my wonder and admiration. This was, no doubt, a faithful representation of that period. But even in the Land of Puritans this good old custom of the fathers seems to be, "More honored in the breach then in the observance."[2]

Somehow mankind seems to require the scourge and the lash. The great religious revival in the far north was preceded by a distressing famine

2   Shakespeare's *Hamlet* (Act 1, scene 4).

in that country. The earthquake in California set on foot a movement for the abolition of the saloon system. While similar distresses in other parts of this country have caused the "Lion and the Lamb" to lie down together, material prosperity seems to blind men's eyes, and they forget to "Praise God from whom all blessings flow."[3]

Strolling along one day I came upon a neat and substantial edifice. "What church is that?" I asked of an old man who lived nearby.[4]

This ancient was more than eighty years of age. Obligingly he told me the name of the church. "You must have a large congregation."

"No, the number of persons who attended this church when I was young and occupied places reserved for the choir, alone outnumbered the entire congregation that meet here now for worship at irregular intervals," he answered sadly.

There are to be found however, many types of the "Village Preacher,"

"A man he was to all the country dear,
And passing rich on forty pounds a year."

for I fell sick, and such a person with his good wife drove six miles, through a snowstorm to bring me words of hope and consolation.[5] In common with those in other parts of our beautiful land, there are many who hope and pray for, and confidently look forward to a great religious revival. To that end let all join, at least reverently in spirit, in the old plantation hymn:—

"Gib me dat old time religion
For 'tis good een de time ob trouble,
'Tis good wen de doctah gib me ober
Tis good enuf fer me."[6]

3   The phrase is from a Christian doxology or a common hymn of praise.
4   This elderly neighbor tells him about the church. Remains unnamed.
5   In characterizing the village preacher, Williams quotes a poem titled "The Deserted Village" by Oliver Goldsmith (1770).
6   This song was listed at least as early as 1873 as one known to be sung by the Fisk University Jubilee singers, but it later evolved to be an extraordinarily popular Southern Gospel standard.

It was summer when I arrived in Springlake, but as I remarked before, summer does not linger here. It was soon haying-time; a very busy season of the year. They had hardly gotten the last load from the meadow before snow came! The snow seemed beautiful—nay, 'tis beautiful. To get the full effects of its beauty you should be in a nice warm room looking out at it through double panes of glass. For, if you have to shovel a half mile through snow three feet deep, you are apt, if you are not a very temperate man, to find yourself using strong and uncomplimentary terms in reference to the poets who sing of its loveliness.

It was my duty to shovel snow; I who had never seen snow more than two or three times in my life before, and at that only an inch or two thick. I had to run the furnace, too. This latter was more to my liking. One day I was sent on an errand during a snowstorm. My way lay down grade, but I went heedlessly on chanting gaily, "Where the snowflakes fall thickest, nothing can freeze."[7]

I had begun to have some misgivings though, for while the flakes were falling thick and fast, I was already half frozen. Some minutes later I knew nothing at all, for down I went, striking my head against a rock. The little Eva of the household was playing out in the storm with the thermometer about twenty degrees below zero, just as happy as are South Carolinian children when they go out gathering jasmines in May.[8] She ran to my assistance, helped me to rise, and led me back to the house. I was stunned and dazed.

When I regained consciousness they were bathing an ugly cut on my head, from which the blood poured profusely. I had relied on Mr. Holmes. I knew he was a humorist, but I confess I had taken him seriously. I cost me about half a gallon of good warm southern blood to discover that he was only joking, for frequently under a very heavy covering of snow, there is a bed of ice as smooth as glass. This is put there by the intelligent New Englander to impart that glad movement to his sleigh, which is so entrancing when he goes out driving with his best girl.

7   Oliver Wendall Holmes's poem, "The Boys."
8   Little Eva was the name of an angelic young child featured in Harriet Beecher Stowe's *Uncle Tom's Cabin*.

One day when it was very slippery the laundress went out to the clothesline. She was in danger of falling. The chivalry of South Carolina was upon me. I rushed to her assistance, and down I went at her feet. I was in a splendid position to propose, but being already married I refrained. "Arise brave knight," said the lady, "They at the castle doth laugh at us."

My employer was an energetic man. He had built a house on a rock;—rather on the place where a rock used to be. "How are you ever going to build a house on that rock?" he was once asked. Napoleon like—he answered, "There shall be no rock," and straightway began blasting. The result was, a palatial mansion that towers above the surrounding houses, as the owner does above ordinary men in energy and determination. Such a man as he had no time to waste on a "tenderfoot" from South Carolina, therefore, "When the gentle springtime came" he told me I had better return to the sunny south; offering very kindly to arrange for my return passage.[9] But, like the noble Frenchman, I said, "Here I am and here I stay."[10] That is, I declined his offer with thanks.

"What are you going to do?" he asked.

"Work, sir," I replied.

He looked at me with incredulous smile. There was one however, whose kindness I shall never forget. One who had not altogether lost confidence in me, and through whose kind intercession I obtained another situation. By this time I had become "inoculated," and was able to give entire satisfaction to my employers, who were also very kind gentlemen.[11]

The little town of Springlake (you won't find it on a map, for it is hidden away between high mountains), is a most beautiful and a typical New England settlement. Nature has done wonders to beautify the place. Some one has said the Garden of Eden was in the United States. If it were not for the fact that the mercury frequently falls to forty degrees below

9   This is a quotation from "A Wonder Story," a poem by Mary Frances Hall, published in Mary Frances Hall, *Story Land: A Second Reader* (New York, Globe School Book Co., 1901), pp. 197–202.

10   Williams is continuing his reference to Napoleon here.

11   Williams uses "inoculated" here, but evidently means that he has become accustomed to the brutal weather conditions of Vermont winters.

zero, and that the summer passes like a "watch in the night," I would be inclined to believe that this is the place.[12]

The people of Springlake—well, they are New England people; and that is all that need be said. The women are of course, better than the men, as is the case all over the world.

---

12   "A watch in the night" is a common phrase he is probably lifting from the King James Bible, Psalms 90:4. Here he uses it to suggest that summer passes so quickly that it is almost an insignificant event.

CHAPTER XVIII

Wrong Impressions

"Twix Twiddledum and Twiddledee."[1]

In many parts of New England a very erroneous impression prevails regarding the attitude of the white people; I mean the white people of the south toward the Negro. The general idea seems to be that the average southern white man sallies forth every morning with a bowie knife between his teeth, and the first Negro he meets, proceeds to lay him open in the back, broil him on a bed of hot coals and thus whet his appetite for breakfast. I found too, that this impression is largely the result of the thoughtlessness and altogether unnecessary talk of many southerners visiting the North, who seem to feel it incumbent on them to disavow the very friendly relations that exist between these two races in many parts of the South, by expressions of indifference, and intolerance, that in many

---

1   While "Tweedledum and Tweedledee" are commonly known as nonsensical and quarrelsome twins in Lewis Carroll's *Through the Looking Glass and What Alice Found There* (1871), the characters come from nursery rhymes of an earlier era and unknown origins. The phrase is often used as a shorthand for choosing between two equally foolish and unattractive choices—usually people who act in identical ways. Here Williams appears to suggest that there are problems in the South and also in the North when it comes to attitudes towards race and practices of racism and that geography is not the determiner of cruelty.

instances are never manifested at home. The northerners do not under-stand that these expressions are only meant in a sort of "Pickwickian" sense; hence the error.[2]

There is a northern family, a branch of which lives in Dixie, who, before the war were large owners of slaves. Some years after the war, a member of the southern branch visited relatives in the North. In answer to one of the children as to how their slaves had been treated he replied, "Oh we treated them about the same as we did our horses and mules."

Such expressions do no possible good, and are frequently productive of harm. As a matter of fact, the southern family was noted for the very humane manner in which they treated their slaves, and some of those old servants as well as the descendants of others, are in the service of the family at this very day.

Again, the little girl who had asked this question was asked by one of the servants, how she liked her southern relative. "Not one bit," she replied, "I can never like anyone who speaks of treating people like cattle."

"My father once shot ten of his slaves. Yes sir, shot them down in their tracks because he thought they were planning to run away!" and the young "Munchausen" from the South, looked around with an air of superiority on the Yankee youths to whom he was speaking.[3]

Somehow the impression has gotten abroad that the ordinary form used by the southern white people in addressing a Negro is "nigger." Now, it is well known that this term is never used by the better class, for, "Though I be a native here and to the manner born," I can truthfully say I have never, in a lifetime of fifty years, once had the term applied to me personally; and curiously enough, the only time I ever was offended

2   "Pickwickian" comes from Charles Dickens's *Pickwick Papers* and refers to friends who insult one another but whose words are not meant to be taken literally. The adjective is used here to imply that the Northerners are not under-standing that these statements about the poor treatment of slaves are deliberately aberrant and should not be taken in a literal or serious manner.

3   "Munchausen" is a common nineteenth- and twentieth-century term for liars that entered the language from a mendacious character in the German writer Rudolf Erich Raspe's 1785 book, *Baron Munchausen's Narrative of his Marvellous Travels and Campaigns in Russia*, later popularized by all sorts of folkloric and popular cultural iterations.

by it happened in the North.[4] (This of course, was not at Springlake). At this time I was employed at a large store in a country town. One day a farmer came into the store. Now when I was a little boy a kind lady school teacher from New England had given me a little book that contained the picture of the Yankee Overseer on a southern plantation, "Who down in the South became whipper of slaves."[5] Upon seeing this farmer I thought that picture must have been taken from life, for he bore such a remarkable likeness to it.

"Whar's your nigger?" he asked, speaking to one of the clerks, "I got some pertaters I want him to help unload."

I had a good place, but I made up my mind that before I gave him any assistance, I would throw up the job. Therefore I went on with my work, and he got his load off without any help from me.

The term "nigger" is a much controverted one. There is not the slightest doubt that it is offensive to all intelligent, self-respecting Negroes, and is never used by them. This term like any other, without regard to their significance or lack of significance, becomes offensive when applied in derision. And, as has been the case with many other terms, thus applied will lose its offensiveness in proportion, as the object it shall secure the respect of those by whom it is applied.

I can not tell of all I saw and of all I learned in New England: of industry, of economy, of thrift, of wealth, of charity. It is a goodly land, and yet,

> "I love the land where the cotton plant grows,
>   The land where there is no ice.
> I love the land where the jasmine blows
>   I love the land of rice."[6]

---

4   Shakespeare's *Hamlet* (Act 5, scene 4).

5   While the quotation is of unknown origin, the broader reference here is most likely to Simon Legree, the infamous Yankee overseer who violently abused enslaved people in Harriet Beecher Stowe's *Uncle Tom's Cabin*.

6   These verses might be a play on the song by Daniel Decatur Emmett, usually known as "I Wish I Was in Dixie," but it might be from another popular verse or song that has yet to be identified.

Both north and south, ours is a great land, and we are justly proud of it. I say "we" and "ours" for I know not what else to say. When I am in the South I feel at home, and as I gaze on the high hills and lofty mountains of New England, I feel as ready to sing "My country 'tis of thee—" as any man in America, for notwithstanding the untoward conditions surrounding my people in many parts of this land, the heart of the Negro is loyal.[7]

"Send him away," say some. "God forbid it!" say I. But, if that sad day should ever come, let the Negro fold his arms. The great fear is that this people are looking in one direction while going in another. The danger is that they may run against a wall.

The financial, the labor, the agricultural, and even the "servant girl" problems have been discussed pro and con very thoroughly. There is one problem, however, that does not seem to receive the attention its gravity demands.

Divorces have reached an alarming proportion in some parts of the United States. It is noteworthy that they so frequently occur where the sexes appear to possess in even measure, those qualities that would seem to make them of mutual assistance to each other, and where similar educational advantages should render them mutually agreeable.

The separations too, are often sought on grounds which look ridiculously inadequate. For instance; Because breakfast was not ready promptly at fifty-seven minutes after six o'clock, on the one side, or some equally grave offense on the other side. Were I called upon to say what, in my judgment, are the strongest forces at work to undermine the foundation of this great Republic, I should name, lynching and divorce.

I for one, have no fear for the ultimate fate of the Negro. My fears are for the American nation, for, I feel as an American, and cannot feel otherwise.

---

7   These lyrics are from "America," a patriotic song penned by Samuel Francis Smith in 1832, often known as "My Country, 'Tis of Thee," sung to the tune of the British national anthem "God Save the Queen."

Index